The Bitches Door

Brazell Tornellini

FIRST EDITION

©opyright 2015 by Brazell Tornellini

All rights reserved. No part of this publication may be reproduced or transmitted in any form or by any means, electronic or mechanical, including photocopy, recording, or any information storage and retrieval system, known or unknown, without permission in writing from the publisher. Address all inquiries to the Publisher.

ISBN-10: 0692571728
ISBN-13: 978-0692571729 (Drury's Publishing)

Gary Drury Publishing Ministries ©™

Produced in The United States of America.

DEDICATION

To emotional bitches

CONTENTS

Dedication	07
Preface	23
Prayer	27
Coup De Grace	29
Youthful Hunger	30
Master	31
Crawl	32
Immortality	33
Hell's Paradise	34
Desiring Needs	35
Meticulously Soul	37
Until Another	38
Dream Souls	38
Thy Neighbors	39
The Unity of the Living Dead	41
Bittersweet Memories	42
Gaza's Chaos	43
Coat of Rainbow Colors	44
My Bad	45
Crazy	56
Abortion Woes	57
Vanishing	59
Justice	50

Survivor	51
One Nation	52
QUEST the FIRE	53
The War Is on . . .	54
The Thin Red Sun	56
OH LORD and SATAN	57
I Miss I Be She	59
Rapido Vogue	61
Crimson Red	63
My Heart's Your Home	65
My House	67
Bow Wow Wow	68
Free	69
Secrets	69
Wondering Streak	70
Have and to Hold	71
Keep Driving	72
Winter Snow	74
Thorn in My Flesh	76
Fire	77
Eye of the Beholder	78
Original Sin	80
Last Directive	81
Proclivities	82
Shadows	83
Only to	83
Little Lamb	84

My Christmas List	85
Wizardry	87
Purgatory's Child	88
Erase My Love	90
Kisses Fall	91
Love Has No Face	92
As the Rain Falls	93
My Resurrection	94
Liberty	96
Man	97
Woman	97
Procula	98
Withering Heart	99
What Be My Crime?	101
Gentle Rain	102
A Colorful Corpse	103
— Behold —	
— Incubating —	
— Now —	
— Charlie Manson —	
— a Gypsy's Soul Fought —	
— This Be Not the End —	
— the End Must One Day Come —	
— T.o.n.e. —	
— I Need Not Dwell —	
Gilded	111
Jackals	112

Fallacies	113
Elegant	115
Volcanoes Fire	116
One Man's Stand	116
Contempt	117
Seasoned	118
Eyes of Desire	119
Fables	119
When We Met	120
Elegant Night	121
Barren Roads	122
Two as One	123
Showering	124
Alone Not Lonely	125
Release	125
The God within	126
Past Midnight	127
Delinquent	130
Frozen Air	131
Connotate	133
Bible	134
Desireé	135
Catastrophe	136
Rage & Disguise	136
Acerbate	137
Asphyxiation	138
Midnight Jesus	139

Raven	141
Haunting Secrets	142
Excavation	143
My Chiseled Body Wilts	144
Whaling Tides	145
Hurricane	146
Flying Thing	147
Whirlwind	147
No	148
Magnificent Dance	149
Two Hands	150
Finding Sight	151
Paige	152
Witching Hour	153
Gravity	154
Ireland Grass	154
Libation	155
Stillness	156
Perhaps	157
In a Sea of	158
Termination	159
Wisdom's Heart	163
Tortured Path	163
Sin and Failure	164
Handsome	165
Rushin' Tears	166
In the Pause	167

Small Town	169
Tequila Cocktail	170
Barring My Soul	171
Running	172
Facade	172
Hold	173
Deep Black	174
Will Be Strong	175
Sculpted	177
Think 'Bout It	179
Season Greetings	179
In Time	180
Deepest Pain	181
Ravages of Time	182
You Have No Name	183
Mister Digital	184
Touch My Heart	186
Strange World	188
Haven House	189
Dead Soul	190
In a World so Small	192
Why Can't I See	193
In This World	195
Country Boy Blues	197
Into the Night	199
Hard Lace	200
Part II	

Masquerade of Nightly Woes

Part III

Wisdom

Cowboys Are Loners	214
Cowboys Don't Rockin' Roll	216
Moment of Pause	217
Come Day, Come Night	218
Magical Words	220
Where Would You like My Body	221
Voices	222
Blue Eyes	223
Cowboys Are Rugged Men	224
Lyrics and Memories II	226
Friend	228
Reality	229
In the Rain	229
I Have No Love	230
Imagine	231
Little Lamb	232
One Man Walking Alone	233
Normally	235
Wild Cowboys	236
Pretty Boy Cowboy	237
Lonesome Stranger	239
Like	240
Waiver	242
Hillbilly Heck Backwards Town	244

Fastidiously Perfect	245
I Am Walt Whitman	246
I'll Not Apologize	247
Seasons of Hell	248
Yearning	254
God's Abide	255
You're My Love Elixir	256
Wildly Madly Deeply True	257
Tarzan Is a Friend of Mine	258
Porous Night	260
I Am	261
Deep Penetrating Emotion	263
Paramount	264
There Was a Time	265
Spring Has Sprung	266
Fur Elise	267
When I'm Gone	268
Run It Hard	269
Broad Stroke	270
Virus Disease	271
Intrinsic Nature	272
Forever Hibernate	273
Troubled Soul	275
Phantom Love	276
Finally	277
Dirty Little Secrets	279
Love Me Now	280

Men with Broken Hearts	281
The Fires of My Heart	283
Colors of All Hues	284
Blacken Dirt	285
Suicide Was Close by	286
Primary	287
Low Dragon Fumes	288
Inter Wounds	290
Just Walk on by	291
Recalling Memories	291
Waterfall	292
Occasions Wisdom	294
Dragon	297
Satellite Eye	298
I Am Blind	299
The Dead Commit to Sin	300
Taste My Kiss	302
At A Masquerade Ball	303
Dropping Shadows	304
Enchanting Charms	305
Caravan	309
Hear the Love	310
Unfinished	311
Neither Here nor There	312
Nocturnal	313
Consequences	314
Skeleton Bones	315

Senses	316
Procession	317
Color My Soul	319
Barren Run	320
Struck Hard by Fate	321
An Urn's Just Fine	323
Four Walls	324
Nearly Alive	325
Vacant	326
Silvery Tongue	329
Stone Hearts	330
Way Ward Child	331
Simple Soul	332
Corpse	334
Idol Hands	334
Light	334
Chambers	335
Dragonflies	335
Sounds	336
Grave	336
In the Name	327
Witness	338
Contemplative Prose	341
Loose Thoughts	342
Beyond the Stone	343
Drowning in a Sea of My Memories	345
A Sight to Blind	347

Dead to Speak	348
Pray to My Shadow	349
Fragments	350
Home Is in My Heart	352
No Friend of Mine	354
Half a World	355
Collegiate	356
Days of —	357
Silent Mirror of Memories	358
That's How I Roll	359
Faceless Words	360
Blank	362
The past Resolved	363
Kentucky Clay	364

PREFACE

Poetry is an art form using a palette of words to color an imaginative scene in your mind as you read each condensed story whether it is abstract or literal. This gentle writing offers artistic expression and self-therapy as it cleanses the mind permitting the creative muse to dance in total freedom. I express myself freely in this medium on any given moment of time and mood. I make no apologies as I indulge in this creative release. Many writers elect to enjoy third person while I prefer to use first person the majority of time just to immerse readers into these rendered worlds. Capturing an essence of truth rarely conveyed in a politically correct environment. Each poem is a star, a planet, a comet, stardust residing in my vast universe of uncharted galaxies.

Before the court of literary reverence I have stood accused on plethora occasions for romanticizing suicide which I make no apologies for as this is not the intent. I merely indulge in the mysteries of what may be awaiting in the hereafter dancing around and momentarily upon the border of imaginative discovery. It is anyone's guess as to the masquerade pending in continual question between limbo and purgatory.

A plethora of poems gracing these pages touch on a variety of subjects and constructed in several different styles appeasing the most discerning of intellectual desires. If even one poem fails to ignite some form of emotion whether it be disapproval, hate or sadness then I have not succeeded in my endeavor. However, when day closes and the sun kisses the earth on horizon the only person I need to appease to achieve success is "I". The rest is just your own Heaven or Hell grounds on which you must battle.

Some poems though separate compliment additional poems within this collection. For every lock there is a key–!

PRAYER

I am endangered, Sir,
I know not now,
What I may retrieve from my thoughts
That venture to seek all
That is and will soon be
relentless is my universal soul
searching
reaching
Toward a way to be set free
From the darkness
Restlessly still
That leaves it boundlessly trekking
in the directional flow of a carousel
Where my soul stagnates and swells
Pondering its eternal hell.

There is no sign in the blue hue skies
To signify this will soon end
An I,
Like the winds of a tempest storm
Cannot bend the forest for the tree
Standing firmly in the way.

You, Sir, can lead the way
Blazing a fiery path
With your mighty staff
To lift my soul
Away from its desolate hell
of loneliness and despair
This I say in prayer

coup de grace

True forgiveness comes unconditionally
from the soul
Or else, belongs to a union dead.

Gallantly rushing the stiffness of the pace
As I swiftly move without a glimmering of trace,
To all, I bare my wickedly pale face.

Then, the fiery red season approaches
Covered in a lily-white
Called snow
— A season without a heaven
— A season without a hell
— A season where religion
      plagues the unsuspecting
Gullible in primitive ignorance,
Magical thinking,
Disguised as wisdom
To the soul

Alas! Alas! Coup de grace.
Alas! Alas! A death blow.

YOUTHFUL HUNGER

How luscious is the youthful vintage rose?
Before thee
That has been forbidden from my taste
As the pangs of hunger heaving pain within
Grows grows and grows
Within the solemn depths of my soul.

With each drudging step of a passing day
Longer, immeasurably longer than the last
Though shorter than the next
I do confess.

I await the taste of its sour sweetness
On the tiniest of my swollen taste buds
embedded upon my mortal tongue.

Waiting for the last
In Spring
Rising above the rest.

MASTER

I as current flow bi-directionally through the circuits
Of my destiny
Labeled: LIFE.

Amplifying as I pass swiftly through each stage
That is so neatly packaged with copper paths
Are indigenously ignored by my preconceived master
Awaiting new input to improve or destroy
Or repeat indefinitely
My own in this era.

Extended memory is continually being installed
Intended desire
For retaining additional data
Matriculating computations
Instantaneous recall can bottleneck
As I add another vintage year
To what resembles my life.

Then, I give my last and final stroke
To the black ivory QWERTY keys
That sustains and comforts me.

CRAWL

Crawl inward the bent mind
Through my sun struck eyes
Where you shall see in one moment

    — no love, no hate
    — no fear, no life
    — no death —

But, a darken world of scarlet red.

Nothingness, you shall swear
By your God
You have entered this hell
Like there is no other.

I can relieve myself of this vacant shell
— SUFFERING —
From all that will always be,
From all that shall never be.

A point
Where movement does not stop
Nor does it move
It's merely positioned in time.

IMMORTALITY

It shall be so sinfully delicious
But society appallingly screams NO!
Yet, my mind and flesh screams
Infinitely – YES!
When chance prevails
Opportunity knocks
Upon my chamber door, again.

I shall taste the juices of life
Inundated, filled with zest and immortality.

HELL'S PARADISE

Vicariously, I fell into this grace
Which is indigenous to my race.

Endogenously, I wrapped my body
In pretended mortality;
While
Seeking all that is and was
And will soon be.

Impetuously, I searched for more to
Inundate my desires
Luring in my present, future grasp
Platonic I and my desires shall never be
For promiscuous are these human deeds.

I defined are Hell's paradise.

DESIRING NEEDS

Musically she dances across the night
In her translucent sheer lace negligee
Allowing moonlight to stream through
As she passes me with her bewitching smile
In front, she stands devilishly enticing
By an open bay window leering
Looking like a white wing dove in silhouette.

Creating a thirst in my flaming heart
That tantalized the fiery taste buds of my soul
Desiring to be quenched
By her sweet warm juices of life.

Her soft golden skin burns of fire
When our throbbing flesh touches
With un controlling purgatory flames
Feeding the desires of our lust
Quenching a thirst that has been
Unquenched for so long, so long

Again, our fevered flesh burns
Unable to translate into intelligible words
These of our two souls are set fees.
As the nectar of life baths, us in its ecliptic moment
Alas!

This from the tangled web of one glorious night
We find ourselves betrothed to desire
Moving onto the next taste of heaven's delight
To fill more of our earthly desiring needs.

METICULOUSLY SOUL

Movement
Is a meticulously graceful skill
Instilled in my manly race
With charisma
That illuminates a transmitted
Wash
Alluring potential items
Emitting
An unquenchable desire for lust
Sensuous seductive charm
Compelling and intimate
Hunger of attraction
Awaiting to be satisfied
With a flavorful kick
Awaiting to be savored
When the nectar flows
Our souls warm.

UNTIL ANOTHER

I have a provocative piquant dwelling within as my lost wondering soul units with another — it becomes burning flesh that volcanically erupts, consummating my non-platonic interlude — soiling the soul tastefully with sin — Lusciously so.

DREAM SOULS

Undead tales of lost horror stories inundates our simple minds,
relentlessly contriving to indulge in the mundane —
of frolic activity.

No valid substance of sour inquisitive taint the mind,
the same way as undead tales, leading them and
I to un serene and violent waters waving with the wash of acid.

Acid wash frolic cleanses the logic from our minds
That it may pursue a liberal focus of creativity —
on the last variable edge.

Eager to entice and hypnotize dream souls.

THY NEIGHBORS

Thy neighbors are as strange as they can be
Doors are shut, shades are drawn,
With lights on day long
Off at nightfall.

They creep about in silent shout,
With windows, open wide
You can hear the children's screams
Flowing through the screens.

Doors open yet? Nothings there, I swear!
Stand back — BEWARE,
Doors slam shut, all so tight
In the mid of night
Whatever was there
Used much of its might.

They walk about through each room,
Doorknobs removed
They lost their screws
I see them carrying something
It's a dead child from their torture room.

The neighbors are leaving now,
Making a lot of sounds
To where they're going—
It won't be long — they'll be back soon
There are more children in their torture room.

My neighbors living in a brick house
On suburban street
Their caged as if they are laboratory mice
From all the drugs that they are on
needing their brains spliced
To ease their lobotomy.

THE UNITY OF THE LIVING DEAD

A pretty cardinal,

Ran into the black raven,

The colorful corpse,

Played,

The singing bird,

For the unity of the living dead.

BITTERSWEET MEMORIES

If I should stay,
I will only bring you misery and pain
A pain, that I can never erase
My time has come to say goodbye
"Please don't cry"
"Please don't cry"

Bittersweet memories
Are locked within my heart
I'll keep them close, inside
As I watch over you from afar
Soon the time will heal my scars
I'll treasure you in my heart
For all eternity, for all eternity

We both know what the other feels,
Time will heal our wounds
Let me see your face, light with a smile
Remember me in your special way,
"I'll always love you,
This you will always know."
The taste of bittersweet memories

GAZA'S CHAOS

Gaza's chaos ignites and sustains
The wealth of life's treasures
The times we have shared
Can never be truly measured
No amount of money can compare
To love, I have for you

Wings flutter and a tear sighs
For the passions burning inside
Our time is inundated with pride
With you hand and hand by my side

Gaza's chaos keeps us alive
Holding our fires high
As our love continues to fly
In a world where we never die

I will always love you.

COAT OF RAINBOW COLORS

Wrapped in my coat of rainbow colors
I hold all of life's treasures freely
In the midst of this colorful light
My sadness washed away with delight

But, the ticking of each small grain of sand
Erodes away the joy we shared across this land
In my deepest, direst times of need
My Guardian angel, have you forsaken me?

When I had given in to the sin
Of suicidal tendencies, a voice wisped by
An in your shadow, I felt your love
Blanketing me in a coat of rainbow colors
Wiping away my tears as . . . I cried

My spirit lifted to heaven's above
Praising every glorious moment of love
Shrouded by angels far and wide
In my coat of rainbow colors,
You stand there by my side

MY BAD

Sometimes the truth is best when it's permitted to hide.
A little white lie is best when it patches those feelings inside.
This you did not realize until you felt the crushing waves collide.
Life is inundated with ups and downs that continually bind.
Time is limited don't fool around and let things eternally slide.
Endeavor to prosper and success will be favorably abound inside.

    My bad, my bad,—For letting the truth come out.
    My bad, my bad,—For allowing the silence to shout.

Don't ruin your life merely to be a clown who forever abides.
Groom your integrity and character and walk in solemn pride.
This you will realize in despair as you feel the crushing waves collide.

Sometimes the truth doesn't arbitrate a right or wrong side.
A balance in life can be difficult to mediate when the string is tied.
This you cannot contemplate until you've felt
    the crushing waves collide.
This is the tragedy, the comedy, the romance, and the thriller of time.
As God sets the stage for your free will, you matriculate
    in your own demise.
Forgo the shadows and stroll in the luminous light
    where truth does hypnotize.

CRAZY

I'm must be crazy to keep you around
But you're the only one that turns my frown
Upside down

Crazy Jolene
Your devilish walk
and flaming stare
is beyond compare
I'll crown you queen
Of my land
Stand with me
As king and queen
Before each man

ABORTION WOES

Weep not for me my child
But for your children and theirs
For the hours are drawing near
Where pestilence, disease, and decay
Shall lay a blacken path of waste and devastation
In the wakeful eye of the new world order this day.

Weep not for me my child
My heart is not pure like theirs
For a time, has drawn me near
Where nothing, nothing strays
The path is open wide for all obliteration
In my watchful eye, I witness the Armageddon.

Weep not for me my child
My hand and forehead are bare
I need not of material things
In the chaos where digital rings
Your number has been called
Fall to your knees child, fall.

Weep not for me my child
I'm no longer digitally bound
To the ways of gated Earth
The awakening or the rebirth
The golden trail narrows multiplying your crime
In my watchful eye, I bear witness to —

    The rebirth of Destiny's Child

VANISHING

Starring out the window of hopeless despair
With a picture framed of you standing there
My thoughts gradually vanish into the harshness of night
My eyes are giving way to the vanishing light

The sky is of grayish hue and the grasses of bland green
Trees towering my mortal head appear much to lean
I needn't test wills or put up a fight
My eyes are giving way to the vanishing sight

With a broken spirit and a mournful heart
It will be a resurrected life to start
Will my mind wander away, destined to this plight?
My eyes are giving way to this vanishing life.

My heart rains with severe toil and pain
Awaiting a rebirth inundated with sprite – aim
A silhouette undistinguished takes flight
My eyes are giving way to the vanishing night

JUSTICE

Blinded by darkness and devilish delights
Crime is on a rampage like a disease and a plight
No responsibilities tucked away out of sight
Justice is an unfounded freedom clutter with rights

Digitally bound to conspiracies and wavering edicts
Perpetual motion will usher in prophets to predict
Fallen angels and winged things savor all derelicts
Justice will abide by the greed of one governing district

Justice aids the plentiful avenues of dread
Seizing the moment to galantine one's head
With head floating in a bucket of blood
Society condolences engross the distance of love

Enchanting charms cloak and scales
Withering the weary violently pale
Energies soar and gather to new heights
Digitally bound to impale and force a fight

SURVIVOR

Tropical storms gather and oceans heave
Twisting and mangling a steel ship with ease
Instantly there's nothing in sight but bobbing heads
Survivors washing to shore with hearts filled with dread

Peering eyes and hungry souls
Stirs aggression for immunity pose
Tribal gatherings partake the dance
To remain whole or forgo the chance

Tropical storms linger and take their hold
Escalating tempers, uncovering the moles
Shelters collapsing of leaves and sticks
What they would all give for mortar and bricks

Physical strength and ingenious processes flow
Focusing the wading tribe of leery warriors tow
Gathering prowess primes the survivor soul's
As one fertile seed begets edicts that prosper and grows

It's a chance in a million to take home the prize
Everyone will befriend you with deceit and lies
Leery are those who play the game wise
Only one man takes home the million-dollar grand prize

ONE NATION

Place your money on the mark
Test my love, if you don't trust yourself from the start
It's midnight dark, the stakes are high
It's you and me, one on one.

Gray is many shades, Guilt is a sharp blade
Edging toward danger . . . One wrong move —
Both our worlds divide, Leaving us in a daze.

Hear silent music humming in the mist
The construction has begun
We're laying the foundation
Just you and I, as one nation
Destine for goodness
We're giving birth to our world's salvation.

It's dark, our souls are day
It's light, our hearts are a million miles away
Entwine, we're one nation
Birth of free will
Wanting, waiting, waiting to be free

Hear silent earth say
"You're united as a single nation.

QUEST the FIRE

I quest the fire waning my hunger
A thirst that habitually never flees
A want, a need
I'd never free my desire.

There's no one way to quench, appease
The blazing fire within won't cease
Though I can't comprehend its matriculation.
When I'm here today and memories reappear
Empty fears loom no more.

In this house, I've restored
As visions of lost memories replay in my mind
Recalling our lofty nights as one
Displays so vivid, I feel my temperature rise.

I quest the fire, living in this dream call reality
Where no one but you relate to me.

THE WAR IS ON . . .

Life and blood are traded in
The war is on
Innocence of violator
Crushed in victory
Though the battles not won
The war is on . . .

Juvenile minds set fire to revolutionary ideals
But the conformity troops march hard onto traditional rules
Another generation to suffer the disease of conformity
While seeking eagerly a system to set them free.

The war wages on
The war is on . . .

Forest trees enclose a fence against outside societies

As they recite — "I pledge allegiance to censorship!"

Another decade, another century
Are traded in and the war is on . . .

Life and blood
Innocence of violator
Arise in victory
Though the battles wage fourth
No one has won.

The war wages on
The war is on . . .

THE THIN RED SUN

Here comes the night again
Another evening with divinities
Masters of this universe and
I'm a slave to their wills.

I venture to the north and
Find myself south
Trekking into the western ground.
Ooops, eastern skies aglow
An eclipse of my heart
lined with the thin red sun.

Walking not before their eyes
Of mysteries and disguise
Everyone here wears a mask
This destine mark of Ide's.

Pillows fluffed, single lights dim
Television on with white noise and
The radio hums distant songs.

But remember without guilt
This time we share
Belongs only to you and me
Beneath the thin red sunrise.

OH, LORD and SATAN

Oh Lord, I just can't resist —
Heaven kneels before my alter
Bearing diamonds, gold and
A mirror image of me.

Oh Satan, I just can't resist —
The fiery flesh wrapping me
In luring temptation and
The other side I see.

Canons of paradise mull twice
These feelings wreathing inside
Melting flesh to flesh
Melting flesh like ice
It's a bodily sacrifice.

Masculine rites,
Iron lust,
Steel body,
I honor thee.

Sculptured physique
Of marble stone
Your touch burns
Passionate and lovingly.

Oh Lord, I worship your praise
As I do thy name . . .
Take me from this icy embrace
Tonight.

To you I give myself
The fires of my race,
Together as one being
Tonight.

Oh Satan, tumbling through the night
Our rain blankets us
Shadows of desire burn
When two laid as one
Faceless before the light
Cloaked in the darkness of shadows of night.

Oh, how sweet this dream, I can't resist
As the battle wages, harsh and long
Mingling our blood, making us one tonight
Melting lust, quenching desires
As our shadows reign, tonight.

I MISS I BE SHE

I speak in song to manly fragments of form
Angels twinkle in misty velvety nights
Where they secretly converse
Feelings of longing for — I Miss I Be She.

I Miss I Be She
She Miss I Be She
He Miss I Be She
You Miss I Be She

My wailing song for diversity lives
In long fresh nights and hollow thoughts
Walking forward on sharp bladed edges
As his tongue blades the adventures of men vortex.

Sacred homes of love relaxing via feelings
With digiting massage with fondling admiration
Desires truthfully flee toward temptation
With honor and courageous dignity.

Sing! Sing! Sing!
I Miss I Be She . . .

Strength boldly stands before natural innocence
Defending its character before newspapers and
Microwave televisions preaching high tech religion.

Sing! Sing! Sing!
I Miss I Be She . . .

RAPIDO VOGUE

Rapido . . .
Rapido . . .
Rapido . . . Vogue

issho no kyoo
together today
decisions face us
uncertainty lies within
there's nothing to do
but get up and face it
straight on, straight on

Rapido . . .
Rapido . . . Vogue

let's dance and party
coz tomorrow's ahead of us
bringing in something new
and Jesus is on his way
I knew he heard me pray

Rapido . . .
Rapido . . . Vogue

he'll drive the dark of doubt away
open my eyes to his light
once I cross the street of destruction
glowing gold the avenue I left so-long-go
Jesus knew I'd find my way.

Rapido Vogue

CRIMSON RED

My eyes are reflective mirrors
Reflections of open windows
Peer deep and penetratingly
Reach in and touch my soul.

I've seen the motley hues inside myself
I reached until I've gone too far
Breaking out of these nightly shadows
My heart crumbles of forgotten stone.

My scene is bloody jaded
Flowing rivers of crimson red
I've followed the sweetest path,
Avenues I've learned to dread.

Trekking in this land of the dead
Until life reached desperately
Grabbing me to sub come to its will
Master, I am thy slave!

I take the pain, the pain you give
I am thy crimson scarlet before your alter
Bare me with your breath of color
Imploring your showering grace.

I take the pain, the pain you give
Dressed in raw flesh and crimson red
This I do for your favor
Should I fall and tread from your grace.

I kneel before thee an implore forgiveness
You are the god I name, the one I kneel to adore
I offer myself in ritual sacrifice at your alter
Drenched in the flavor of blood, crimson red.

For your pleasure, is your meager request
I take the pain, the pain you give
In paradise eating forbidden fruits
There is a world outside these thoughts.

I take the pain, the pain you give
Reach deep . . . reach and touch my soul
Wading in these liquid thoughts of surreal
Reflections are the key to the truth to where I dwell.

MY HEART'S YOUR HOME

Stop, Look and Listen
Pour your sweetest sugar on me
My body is your temple
My heart is your home.

I want a whole lot of trouble with you
Make me drop to thy knees and pray
By no means in a religious way
My heart's your home when we're alone.

I give you my permission
To assume all the wild positions
Where we reside in paradise
Bright eyes we need not advertise.

It's a street some condemn
It's one I highly recommend
As you and I surely comprehend
Life sometimes compromises.

Though life sometimes compromises
A destiny without disguise
Our love will be recognized
Embracing frolic kisses with mysteries and surprises.

My eyes shine bright rays of love
Glowing a heavenly body of stars
A nuclear explosion of a burning sun
Torture in first degree heated above.

Here comes the night draping the world in silence
I raise my chalice to you, I drink from your fountain
Two souls awaiting to become one
Taking advantage of aspirations violating life.

My body is a temple for your undying love
My heart is your home when we lay alone.

MY HOUSE

Here in my house where happiness resides —
Love is comfort,
Beneath this roof where trust is found —
Love is comfort,
In these days where nothing matters —
Love Is a Master in My House.

In this house love, may not always prevail,
Though something good does happen here.
When we're here, here in my house
Everything blends together to bind the two of us.
Love Is a Master in My House
. . . And I Am Its Servant.

No, my eyes aren't filled with stardust and
Experience keeps away memory rust,
But you and I together learn to trust
Magical events between us.
Love Is Master in Our House
Where our love masterly prevails.

To me, some things do matter
As I embrace you and
Cradle you in my warmth.
Like a child
Your heart reaches out and
Your eyes smile at me.
Then I know I found home . . .
Here at my house.

BOW WOW, WOW

Bow wow, wow boy box
Look at blond innocence
Blue eye fox.

Bow wow, wow digital pop
Drowning in mellifluous rain
Driving us all insane — stop!

Bow wow, wow boy box
Bow wow, wow joy rock

FREE

Minds split into halves are free falling
Echoes in the darkness keep calling
Two souls touching in the flesh
Are two souls free, Alas!

SECRETS

Whispers
      seep through my ears
      a telling me things
      I wish to hear,
Secrets.

Whispers
      flow roundabout and
      long the streams of my dreams
      along the while, I hear faint screams, of
Secrets.

Whispers
      inward they move and
      moon-ward they bend
      only to reveal secrets
      that taste like sin.
Secrets . . .

WONDERING STREAK

His touch is sensuously soft with each gliding stroke,
swaying and hanging comfortably around,
his fit is pleasurable, to say the least
in his high-tech style of placement and harmony,
with his art deco and modern philosophies within
his high contemporary tech styles,
that's seen bright for the length of miles,
though there are some who
would not agree or approve,
he's my style, he belongs to me,
no one wears him better than I,
as we pass with a pleasing smile.

But, if you could feel his fit as I do,
you would never let him fade pass,
Because there's nothing more comfortable
then he is my cotton shirt at last.

HAVE AND TO HOLD

Desperate is a minds ache,
suicidal tendencies brake
A soul one forsakes
is a lucky man's fate,
the homeless written slate.

Still, they keep the other in the faith
innocence is the tool,
only one who overlooks
walks like a fool.
Innocence is short-lived
in this modern world
maybe that's why the streets are so full.

Unemployment fills a child's eyes
but, hope and dreams in the heart
keeps them alive
in this suicidal world
trying to hold the innocence of a child
when everything is tumbling of old
Something to embrace memories
something to have and to hold.

KEEP DRIVING

Discover a variety
excitement
what a gay life
anticipating diversity
perversions blackout
bright nights
advocating
rightfully and proud
keep driving
(I'm reaching for the night)
Experts compile comprehensive views,
freelance journalist
provides trustworthy news
response
on a borderline night
keep driving
(Until I find myself.)
Two of a kind
move together protesting
AMERICA
difference searching for
SALVATION
and streetwise religion
plagues humanity
dressing black society

uncovering centuries
DISGUISE
it's all about you and me
the seers who believe
keep
keep driving

WINTER SNOW

In rolled the clouds then came the rains
I listen to the thunder, voices proclaim
freedom is their name.

They were digging a tunnel
through the winter snow and
when they made it through
all the world would know
freedom is their home.

A place of freedom and love
is all that I dream of
in the winter snow and
I the world know
freedom is their name
freedom is their home
when the winter snow came

Standing in the rain watching it turn to snow
soon the thunder dissipated
and the clouds were all gone
and freedom came home
during this winter snow.

It was like a dream in a mother's arms
where everywhere I stood
freedom had made it home,
everyone was happy and warm.

Crystals came falling heavily like rain
soft and cold blanketing everything
showing all who encompass the Earth
who rules all the world
In most of all this winter wonder
people soon began to ponder
the stone wall fell asunder
the staggering cost was a blunder

As the people mingled freely
between east and west
a grand noise echoed across the globe
letting all the world know
freedom is their name
freedom is their home
purified by the winter snow.

THORN IN MY FLESH

Plague
Spot
Evil star
Skeletons
Bare
In the closet.

Ill winds blow a thorn in my side,
Ill winds blow a thorn in my flesh,
Ill winds badly burn — two bodies burn,
Ill winds blow a thorn in my side,
Ill winds blow a thorn in my flesh

The puncture
Inundated with vice
Is the spice of life

Sacred scripts whisper-silent sounds
centuries of history from
one generation to the next
views and opinions change
though the words remain the same
skeptics and believers have much in common,
both retort,
trying to answer
unanswerable questions.

The pain. The agony. The trails. The tribulations.

It's an ill wind blowing a thorn in my side,
It's an ill wind blowing a thorn in my flesh.

FIRE

Fire in her eyes burn with a midnight's disguise
A failed masquerade went awry, my sire
Her body's tied to mine by fire
In a rainbow of colors — feel the power
Whispering sweet nothings and wet sounds
Tonight, the darken heavens glow abound.

Fire from subtle embers strike ablaze
Wrapping rainbows in smoke and haze
Shining like a cosmic heavenly star
Her juvenile kiss with wildflower flair
Ignites a flame burning like a sun
A league of thoughts comes undone.

Fire writhes, scorch, and tingle
Danger lurks in social mingle
Wrapped in rainbows of kissing colors
Superstars display discarded lovers
Washing juvenile thoughts in scarlet dire
Everyone desires their hearts on fire.

EYE OF THE BEHOLDER

Color my soul masquerade
In gay chaos like the winds of night
I'll harbor no ill feelings
Do not procrastinate
Avoid all redundancies
Mellifluous is my amour
Where mundane frolic and trivialities
Are my exotic splendor
Bathing me in a calm wealth of hues
A delight cascading of your essence
Thunderously showering upon thee a paradise
Where only angels dare to tread

I masquerade am the eye of the beholder
Fighting battles and waging wars
Amidst the violent chaos swirling through the night
I'll bear no compunction for your demise
Feverishly I campaign for the subscription of your amour
Prolific be the literacy of thy faithful requisition
Mellifluous is your amour that engrosses thee
Where mundane frolic and trivialities
Bequeath me the bathing calm of your ocean blue eyes
Demons soar deep within my willful soul eager to appease
A thirst that is unquenchable in your drowning essence
Where only angels dare to reside

Thunder roars, lightning strikes this ecliptic day of night
In the midst of all wonder and devilish disguise
Masquerade the only desire in my ravenous eyes
Procrastinate not this winged night
Avoid redundancies, ignore the rite
Mellifluously our amour engages the fight
Where mundane frolic and trivialities
Explore the exotic splendor of our appetite
Eye of the beholder encompass the lore of amour
As the universe expands and contracts
Nourishing the indebtedness of my soul
Where angels are privy to the secrets I hold

Night settles as the dawn begins to waken
Where time stands frozen a mere fraction of seconds
Ecliptic this day of the night — PROCRASTINATE!
Silhouettes merge as one in infinite measure
As paradise bonds two in carnal leisure
Consciousness eludes mortal comprehension
No deed is sought to acquire salvation
Amours rites of passage may be condemned
Paralyzed before heaven's masquerade
Your depth of nourishment appeases carnal cravings
Pouring your angelic rays of masterful delight
Where only angels observe queer nocturnal visions

. . . um . . . what proclivities beseech thee?

ORIGINAL SIN

Adam, Eve, Steve, & Marie
the apple tree
and me to write it all down
spread the word
round, round, round
to all who listen
trapped in original sin.

Original Sin
where it all begins
a place called
PARADISE
with serpents sneaking
offering knowledge
to those who'd listen
offering temptations
sweet temptations.

Holy Father
Holy Mother
Blessed Son
Eve strayed and tasted sin
Adam and Steve listened in
I was born with original sin
Taken away by baptism
Mumbling script with a faithful grin.

LAST DIRECTIVE

Writing is always a poetic adventure for me to express myself and the diversity of my thoughts; which convey simplistic honesty. An endeavor from the sacred valleys of my feverish gray matter with lurking shadows in the midst of wondrous thoughts commonly scaling the ladder of creativity as each synapse ignites inspiration. Oscillating in life's, most valued integration of contemplation and humanist fragments, trekking the boundless and diverse avenues of my venturesome soul. My creations are not idle mundane words and sentences on a virgin sheet of parchment.

My last directive bares the witness to the frolic and regurgitation of enchanting charms, the gay chaos subscriptions to scrupulous detail regulating perfection. Gravely shadowing the crystalline structure of mere mortality, perfection rages war as it lay a single heartbeat away from existence. Yet, it will never be achieved prior to forthcoming generations. Pregnant wisdom looms as the artist holds a pen in hand. What lofty grandeur will offer me the splendor of challenged woes? The most I can endure was achieved in my preceding existence. My duration is limited in this realm as I'm forced to wait for the passage of time.

In this hesitant state of wet ink flows freely my rhetoric without redundancies, no hyperbole graces the last testament of my soul. Closure grants me the remuneration by the longevity of my creations. A gratuity compelled to sustain my last directive.

PROCLIVITIES

Strangely, I'm perched high upon my ivory tower
Draped in the imperial shroud of academia
I pompously direct my gaze upon loyal subjects

Edicts govern their every breath and thought
Proletariats grateful for the morsels bestowed
Eager conformist diligently excavating their graves

As their innate proclivities automate society
Depression and suicidal tendencies abound
With corporations and government appeased

Apocalyptic tribulations are never relinquished
As bearing proclivities endorse the relish woes
Mere wisdom need not elude thy sensibilities

Indulgent needs deteriorate the fevered mind's truth
Bathed in the radiant glory of satisfaction
As digital movement transpire ecstasy

Numbers swarm violently the wealth of chaos
As trivialities collapse asunder to the proclivity
Drink from the chalice of life

    This is my body
    This is my blood
    This is my proclivities

SHADOWS

Among the wake of the day, there are shadows
In the calm death of night, there are shadows
As the ticking of time bears on there are shadows
On an ecliptic day where night resides there are shadows

ONLY TO

Affirmation,
Definition by television
Only to reason.

Appease,
Appendage taste rage
Add vintage
It's only to season.

Anticipation,
Appreciation
Beware destruction
Go on a luncheon
Only to arouse excitement.

LITTLE LAMB

In the name of the Father
and of the Son,
God's little lamb
is on the run
Moving further
toward the burning sun.

MY CHRISTMAS LIST

There is a list of people I know
All written neatly in a book I hold,
And every year around Christmas time
I query it and take a meaningful mind.
This is when I truly realize,
These are not merely names filling my eyes
With joyful tears welling, I tender a look,
They are family and friends not part of a book.
Each one is special like classical art
Each one held in the warmest depths of my heart.

The book of names I hold
Can never be bought or sold,
For each name represents an addition to my life
Each name stands for someone who touched my life.
In that meeting, you became the rhythm of my rhyme,
Nothing can erase the memories of our special times.
We may live distantly or close by
But you are never forgotten in the passage of time
Whether it be by birth or a chance meeting
My Christmas card comes with love and holiday greetings.

Once you are privileged to know someone,
Fond memories can never be undone.
Whether I've known you for several years or a few,
You had a part in shaping the many things I do
Never think my Christmas Cards are mere routine
Of names upon a list forgotten in between
For when I send a Christmas card addressed to you
It's because you are on my list of friends I'm beholden to.
And every year when my Christmas list comes out,
I realize this all anew,
I recall your kind words and friendly face,
All the gatherings and the saying grace.
But the best gift that one can have
Is knowing someone as special as you.
    — Merry Christmas

WIZARDRY

"Wizardry is utter rubbish my lad."
Wiggleton said sternly.
"Pure nonsense."
Stirring over his wired spectacles.

"Simpleton — pinch your pennies, speak proper
And mind your manners."
Wiggleton lectured on.
"But keep these fancy thoughts of fairy tales
Out of your square head.
They'll lead you to no good —
You understand?"

Simpleton nodded meekly,
"I didn't hear that!" Wiggleton exclaimed . . . Did I?"
"I understand sir." Simpleton rolled his eyes as he replies.

"WIZARDRY,
Is for the seasoned scholar to practice.
An untrained lad such as you can do great harm
To yourself and others
Leave it to me and your woes will be diminished.

PURGATORY'S CHILD

When the moon rises so bright
My heart is inundated with fright
As the demon child within takes the night
Your love eludes thee
Imprisoning me to those dirty deeds
Your light finds me on hands and knees.

. . . I'm just a purgatory child.
This is the life you gave
When you abandon thee
You may as well murder thee
And dispose of me
As to abandon me from your love
. . . I'm just a purgatory child.

When night kisses a day
I feel the power you gave
It's a feeling of being saved
Though your love does not constitute my identity
You give meaning to my needs
Your light finds me embracing thee.

. . . I'm just a purgatory child.
This is the life you gave
When you harnessed thee
You may as well liquidate thee
And dispose of me
As to abandon me
  . . . I'm just a purgatory child.

ERASE MY LOVE

Strolling through the gardens,
Following the darkness
To where the sun rests.
Thoughts race through my mind
With each click of passing time.
I feel the terror eroding me
As you erase my love.

No skies above
Heaven falls
I'm in a hell
You don't even care
      You erase my love
        — erase my love
        — erase my love.

My heart hardens
Trickling grains of sand
Swiftly passing by
Remembering treasured kisses
My heart suddenly misses,
A twisting dagger draining
As you erase my love.

No skies above
Heaven falls
Memories recall
An endless love
    — erase my love
    — erase my love
    You erase my love

KISSES FALL

Kisses fall from the sky
Swirling around my heart
Filling me with life
Decimating all strife.

Here comes the rain
Willing a soul of pain
I have no name
On the edge of this plain.

Emptiness consumes my heart
Like a shadow in the night
Kisses fall from the sky
Beseeching miracles on high.

LOVE HAS NO FACE

Love creeps slowly into one's life
You feel so comfortable and warm
In its embrace
But, you never recognize
Until it's too late
Because love is blind
And love has no face.

Love takes you by surprise,
Each and every time,
I relish its delight
But love has a darkness
That invades you like a plague
Much like a cobra's strike
Never do you recognize
Until it's too late
Because love is blind
And love has no face.

AS THE RAIN FALLS

When the rain falls
I hear your voice call
It travels from far away
Amidst the sounds of the day
As the rain falls

The darkness stands tall
And through it, I hear your call
Clear as a seeping blade
Cutting through the night
For this freedom, one must fight
As the rain falls

As the day wakes — then stalls
Upon hearing your sweet calls
And though the thorns of life
Prick and bite
It's the liberty of your love
That holds still my heart
As the rain falls.

MY RESURRECTION

Fine oil paints cascade and flow
A gay palette dries hard but slow
An active scene with winds a blow
From artist hands running hot and cold

I witness my resurrection
Every masterful stroke mere perfection
As I gaze upon passing time
       sustaining my connection
Experiencing the gift of my benediction.

Self-portraits, stills, and landscapes
In a master hands manipulate
Far beyond my words to state
I stand in awe and appreciation.

Its sheer beauty engrosses thee
Bringing me to thy knees
Pleading souls, no demons be
Should time repeat it could be thee.

El Greco — The Resurrection
In dark constitution
Looms of despair without deduction
Salvation is the grand seduction.

Cascading embers of men twist and scream
Blatant cries beyond a dream
One man ascends to be king
Humanity offends, deprived of life's gold ring

Ancient script reintegrates
2000 years of religious debates
Time will shadow the wits of late
To stand back and contemplate.

Fine pigments bright and dull
All chatter falls to a lull
As I peer upon and mull
My resurrection of ancient toil.

LIBERTY

In the cool gentle mist of arbor breeze
My lady stands mightily free
Her torch of glowing embers burn
Reaching the masses that wish to learn
Greeting all with watchful eyes
She held them all close with family ties
She cherishes gatherings
Regardless of language barriers
Welcoming all rich or poor
Her allure is strong for sure

MAN
Bold, Strong
Each holds his own
A masculine rite
A ring to fight

Calm, Alert
A casual flirt
Standing tall
Man, before one and all

WOMAN
Soft, Fragile
Each bears her own
A feminine rite
A wondrous sight

Calculating and stern
A wildfire heart
Standing firm
Woman

PROCULA

Procula rose like the breaking dawn
Full of zest, vigor, and beauty
Casting out her demons of the night
As she embraces the purity of the day

She strolls across exquisite cold marble floors
Adorned in fine linen and romantic stones
As the sun pierces through her open window
Procula welcomes a new day before her gods

Showering before the natural gardens of Eden
The water lovingly ravishes her frail frame
Inhaling deeply and long the airs freshness
Releasing the wickedness impaling her

Servants swarm swiftly with scents and oils
Generously they apply sweet fragrances
Fabrics are carefully laid about
Garments sheer and majestic

Seeking peace from dreams that plague her
She gazed into the stillness of a reflecting pool
Advisory is the wisdom of her truth
A crucifixion indeed looms for sure

WITHERING HEART

Withering heartbeat to a silencing lull
From the last fevered breath of its constitution
Conspiring toward the wealth of sanctuary
Prior to the last drop of tainted blood seeping freedom.

No feeble attempts to ignite a new life
Will sustain the languish eroding my will
Tragedy has struck its dagger firm
Into the depths where the soul dwells.

The withering heart may not witness the break of dawn
The ocean blue heavens or the greenest lawn
As rituals offer closure to the hearts it spawns
Among the fishes in a world's pond.

No idle words will ablaze fresh life
When I lie here barren with decay
Save your script for a surviving soul
Permit my blacken blood to drip away.

The avenues and paths I'm soon to trek
Are cascading with lies and deceit
Darken doorways and beckoning lights
Shall leave me paralyzed with delights.

My excursion may be short and swift
Or I may linger in limbo until eternity
Decisions must be contemplated carefully
As you are all vanishing from my sight.

You all are the validity of my life.

WHAT BE MY CRIME?

Like a shot through the dark
The pain struck my heart
Sheer agony tearing me apart
This news you are giving me
Gnaws with the voracity of terminal disease
How do you deliver such a message with ease?

Like Mozart, we were in elegant tune
Two hearts forever and ever swoon
I never contemplated I'd be losing you
My heart was spirited high
Like a child's helium balloon
Now you are bringing me this hard news.

I inform myself this can't be true
But life's dismantling, there tumble the screws
My only crime was loving you.
When you are near — you are my muse
Without you, my soul merely endures
My only crime was loving you.

Like a shot through the dark — in mid of night
Damaged as server as a lightning bolt strike
The intense pain strangled life right out of my heart
With sincere compunction, I played my part

But you retrieved your dagger and extinguished my light
What ails me now — I have not a cure
What be my crime? — Is my loving you.

GENTLE RAIN

Gentle rain pour down on me
Wash away my guilt and restore my dignity
Gentle rain continues to pour down on me
As virgin light shines upon thee
My mortal heart burns pure you see.

A COLORFUL CORPSE

A colorful corpse
Captures a singing bird
Feeling no compunction
It's all too absurd

Murky hues collide
Shadowing vacancies
Endeavoring sheer perfection
As cascading waters
Rush downward and onward
In a winding, twisting, tryst
Cleansing humans
Worshiping thee

Poetic forgiveness
Appeases a muse delight
Then strong winds gale forth
The breeze fills the blank sail

— *BEHOLD* —

She was the fresh scent of Spring
Fluttering her colorful wings
As her honey dripped sweet and pure
Offering a world of love and rebirth

Bathing in a gentle stream
Crystal waters shimmer and sing
With grasses green, skies sapphire blue
My eyes gleam a hazel hue
Sitting statuette at harp her music swoons

The sun radiates upon her like gods
Never rising and never setting on horizon sod
The universe holds the charms of
Beginning and end within her soul
Captive in freedoms arrest

— *INCUBATING* —

Cultivating my thoughts in flavorful rhythm
Fermenting as they force the surrender
Incubating my words — awaiting new birth
Prolific contemplation gallant and forthright
From the deepest depths of my vivacious soul

A murder of crows winged above
Stark in an aggressive pose
Pressing in an uncertain direction
As queer visions flashed violently my synapses
Like the expiration of one's frail life
When an ingenious thought prevails

My breathing penetratingly shallow
The palpitations of my weary heart hasten
As my frail bones ache naggingly within
Chills waved over my pale alabaster white skin

Something wicked this way comes
Unveiled truths of prophecies
As dead silence froze the surround
The evil cry of hounds initiated echoes

The scent of death draws near
Escalating all heights of fear
Nothing mortal on Earth can measure
Sinners must release all manly treasures

— NOW —

Souls have been sold and lost for less
Desperate constitutions created this ugly mess
Aligning with demons for carnal pleasures
Masquerades collapse, failing unholy endeavors

A murder of crows drop one by one
As death stalks salvations son
Blood rains heavily from Heaven's
Tortured innocence can't be undone
As a colorful corpse missile into the earth's crust

The sacred script loses translation
Through the passages of eroding eras
Latin words of incantation
As excommunicated angels soar
I fall onto my knees in meditation
The transformation of reincarnation
Appeases my metamorphoses

— *CHARLIE MANSON* —

Unholy spirits inundate musky air
Swarming wickedly here and there
Howling, mourning, crying in despair
Enduring agonies plight
The vision of hellish nightmares
reign
My sanity is at wit's end
I need not care or comprehend
I've forsaken the treats of mortal sin
I've to abandon taste of whiskey and gin
Favoring desire that impales my heart
Slowly bleeding the truth of my soul
While my body merely occupies presents
I will not make amends

Strong constitutions wander freely
Uncluttered of sophisticated contemplation
Casually contrived for polite society
Holding army before a battle fought
The war is never artfully won

— *A GYPSY'S SOUL FOUGHT* —

Balancing the immense heavyweight of justice
Is most times a difficult task
Fallacies and illusions entice, certainly
But, the mirror shatters revealing hidden mask
That peer back the truth whaling release
Barren before the chores that task

Blinded by tainted truths
They lawyer-up before the troops
Gambling with each roll of the dice
Justice lifts her blindfold slightly
— at last

Though poetry is a manipulation of chosen words
Creativity is woven to spin a bard
Of heartfelt feelings or injustice
There's no wishing upon a gentle star
As poetry heals and mends my scar
Words are generously constructed one by one

Adding the total, equaling the sum
Each masterpiece sets the Barr
Each masterpiece is second to none

I'll disseminate my creative prose
Page by page, book by book
Across the seas and land
Walking with the dead
Hand in hand
For freedom requires one to take a stand
As the colorful corpse marches on

I've paved this road the scarlet red with my blood
One porous stone at a time
Journeying this glorious land
Because means do not justify the end
I indulged life and love
Despite the communion of sin
Standing proudly before all men

— *THIS BE NOT THE END* —

I've peddled my sacred thoughts on the virgin printed page
In black and white
And all colors in-between

Simple, carefree, with passion and rage
Poetry and prose
Frozen in time but remain uncaged
Ramblings of a madman . . . my sanity saved . . .

Color my soul the hues of rainbows
Inundated with natural treasures showering of gold
Virtual to touch,
memories to have and to hold
The message is simple, conveying the load
When God is answering, the solution is simple
I'm told

— *THE END MUST ONE DAY COME* —

Tis true . . .

You've opened my book
Releasing my words
Good, bad or indifferent
These cryptic messages
Trek onward
Marching into battle
Blood shedding the trenches of war
While my sentences flow
When my sentences lay frozen

— *T.O.N.E.* —

. . . Returning now to your regularly scheduled reading . . .

A colorful corpse
Plays the mute cardinal
Tantalized and marveled
With the spread of masquerade
Of an absurd world

How contrived?
The zombies can't
Distinguish the differences
The facade is feverishly wet
In idle decay and lascivious array
Nemesis need parade the infinite valleys of Hell
As I do in this absurd world

— I need not dwell —

Mere thoughts deduce this nature of course
Disposing of my priceless time
Un worthy to retain their reign beneath
Destiny shall manage fate and
The wealth of wicked tongues

Burn the ventricous fires of Hades
The mechanics of a corpses soul
As synapses divide —

Behold the slivers.

GILDED

Gilded edges gleaming gold
Cherished memories deep in my soul
Abiding edicts I've been told
Tarnished treasures wither old
Amidst a vacant soul
Where angels tread lost and cold
No mere mortal shall ever know
The toil of Heaven as it unfolds
Disseminate the bards told
Across the winds of old
As the story goes.

JACKALS

Listen to jackals' howl carry over wind without scruple.
In the dead of night where souls dare to slumber,
Behind the false security of their chamber doors.
Where their Lord harbors no compunction
For the ills, He bestows upon His peoples.
Something queerly wicked comes in the lull of
Death time strolls beneath a zenith full moon.
Glowing in the embers of twinkling stars and
Blanketed by the deep velvet of night.
No solace will engross a sinful heart
That has withered to oblivion.
As the Sahara Desert composes the wealth
Of a desolate man's morals.
He too must engage the hounds of Hades
Apprentice to Lucifer's reign.
Listen to the fading sounds of jackals
As the sun scorched them away.
They are beyond the salvation of His light.
Drowning in the wickedness of their shackled soul.

FALLACIES

Fallacies parade their dance before my eyes
Suggestive, hypnotic, veiled in disguise
Desiring my participation my constitution abides
Appeasing the hunger growing ravenous with time

Jealousy and rage is an imprisoning cage
Waltzing through Live's wondrous maze
My heart ignites into a thunderous blaze
Consummate my actions ascend the daze

How noble earthy desires be
Entwined in a lover's twist — three be one — as thee
Where fulfilled delights radiate upon my needs
The carriage of justice endeavors to please

No logic or reason dances with fallacies game
As queerly as its wrath melts the cold of Maine
Where mere desires relinquish all blame
For my love is unhindered of any mortal shame

God has forsaken me no answer to my prayers
My voice sails swiftly but found Him nowhere
Coursing the oceans and rivers He is not there
I'm bound alone to do as I dare

Destiny is an illusion guide
Angeled forth to transition the ride
Seldom near or at my side
My masterful hands hold my love untied

Enticing fallacies parade before my eyes
A banquet feast of delights and surprises
And if ever I should need to surmise
My willing heart shall cheerfully abide

For God's heavenly candle's eternal flame
Bears witness to my prayers bellowing His name
And through echoes across the night, my answer came
Not with a whimper or with a roar, but silent and tame

ELEGANT

The elegance of night shimmers in your eyes
Pouring down on me like fine wine
Forcing my heart to die
As my mind goes blind
And the rest of me shivers insane
Before the day draws open unto the light
Presenting truth in vivid sight.

Approach me in the mid of the day
When the sun bathes me with your rays
Forcing my eyes to see
As my heart awakens with joyful sprite
And the rest of my being quivers in your ecstasy
Journey with me prior to the low burning candle flame
Presenting our truth vividly as I speak thy name.

Elegance in the repose of night gleams in your hungry eyes
Showering hard on me like a summer's rain
Forcing my heart to bind
As my mind goes in heavy dark
And the rest of me frozen without shame
As night dances to a close breaking into a fresh light
Presenting truth in a multitude of radiate hues delight.

VOLCANOES FIRE

Nonchalant I stroll into the fire
Eager to bear the heat of desire
For I be as noble as any Sire
When volcanoes regurgitate before one it admires.

Sterling garb of heavy metal
Has weighted strut, so idle settles
In this war of love, I must battle
For volcanoes speak from its boiling kettle.

The fire bubbles, belches, then roar
Spewing smoke and little ash soars
Such a hungry beast desiring more
As volcanoes regurgitate upon the land forevermore.

ONE MAN'S STAND

Disarray floods the logic of wisdom
In a land forsaken of any kingdom
As each man must stand along
In a desert withering him to the bone
Without food, water or wealth
He must reside in stealth
Invisible to all with perfect eyes
For they do not see his slow demise.

CONTEMPT

Where is the contempt I sought today
Generally, it's docked at every bay.
Eager to express its vengeful smirk
Like a cowardly demon, it hither and lurks.
Waiting in the depths of shadows
Preying upon genuinely sincere fellows.

Contempt your contumacy is latent
And your actions are bare and blatant.
Wreathed in sensibilities you're never appeased
You're devastating cancer, a crippling disease.
I'll contemplate not your matriculation
As my pompous disposition ignores your calculations.

SEASONED

Time is running out
A crowd of silence shouts
Bending my mind around you now
Where we find love all around

The season's change
What do they bring
As temperatures rise and fall
In the lull of early Spring
Summer's heat scorch and burns
On heavenly beaches of delight and ocean scenes
Fall leaves of motley hues celebrate
As a choir of birds sings
As winter white settles in,
Bells toll and ring
My love for you is ever stronger
As we do our thing
For destiny, shall be our
Unity and wedding ring

Our initiation has commenced our battling bout
Amidst the righteous and Christian shouts
Bending my mind around such ignorance
I'll never know
Because honorable love is forever bound

Glistening and dancing across ice and snow
While
Shimmering on gale wind crystal waters of tow

EYES OF DESIRE

The kiss of your eyes
Tantalize desires hidden in mine
The words you speak
Hypnotizes to release.

FABLES

Fables are laden in both truth and lies
Tales of darkness and shimmering light
Bards error written or simply revised
A child's heart is destining to decipher the lines
Amidst the monsters and sterling knights
The web of life is revealed in time
As morals and principles are buried in
F – A – B – L –E – S.

WHEN WE MET

When I met you
You opened windows in my soul
Opening me to new horizons
I would have never known
Your beauty be the candy of my eyes
Having you here is my reward and prize
Hypnotize by your soft-spoken words
Not one sentence is left unheard
This romance may not be meant to last
I must appreciate the moment
Give love its chance
To blossom into a splendid thing
Not return it to its desolate weed
Before the chance
When we met

ELEGANT NIGHT

Procession of this elegant night
Slumbered in funeral fairways
Somber reverberation lingered
In frivolous mundane mourning.

When suddenly —

Your eyes shimmered like rippling pools
Pouring down on me like crystal waters
Forcing my heart to arrest and die
As my mind eagerly inundates blindness.

Sterilized by the insanity of this elegant night
I'm compulsively submissive, shivering insane
You have presented truth where love has no name
Before the day draws open unto the light.

Endings must come, but never forgotten —

Procession of this elegant night
Parades beneath the drowning twilight
Eagerly roaring into the new dawn
In celebrations splendor rejoicing.

BARREN ROADS

Barren roads lead everywhere
To distant lands, if my feet carry
An adventure at every turn awaits
Something new, something to learn
For these are the barren roads well-traveled
Tattered and beaten by transmittal mode
Hauling all sorts, I've been told
But I'll not travel these roads today
The road less traveled leads me astray
Now
Its path is narrow and wildly overgrown
The excursion will be hard and slow
But what I'll learn will be shown
Along the road of life
A caters delight is unknown
However rough this journey goes
I'll be the stronger
When I reach, my journeys end
Meeting somewhere at a junction
Kissing a barren road.

TWO AS ONE

Standing firm before splendid ocean view
Sun kisses the earth as night casually settles
Teal waters dance beneath this motley sky,
A fresh stillness encompasses this mode.

The rain has ceased momentarily but lingers in the air
Our umbrella drew us close in a warm embrace
Comfortably, two as one, we inhale the abiding serenity
Heavily lavished before our jaded mortal eyes.

Standing, one squatting the tide strolls in over our feet,
Scruples a moment and returns to rest
We behold such exquisite beauty left unspoiled
As returning rain sprinkles down blessing us.

Taking the other hand we remain two as one
Entwined with shared knowledge of our true love
As the world stands still for mere moments
We are beholden for this precious memory.

SHOWERING

Gushing waters pour worshiping over me
Refreshing, invigorating my weary body
Wading in Eden's fountain pool of youth
I'm revitalized to march forth in battle
Conquering challenges and winning the war
Presented by the task of this modern world

I shall masticate every single living soul
Bare and regurgitate their tainted remains
For my strong muscles, will heave with grand pain
Blood engorged to point of rupture
Aching in barren tribulation for man
Showering shall refresh, invigorate, and revitalize thee

For the drudgery never ceases
A new day initiates the cycle
Again, again, and again
Showering

ALONE NOT LONELY

Head angled down in deep penetrating contemplation
Shoulders square with single-arm behind my back
My stance is approachable without the inconvenience

The stone wall of various hues backdrops my scene
I am alone not lonely as night prowling day-glows
Dripping in eager anticipation adrenaline's euphoria erupts

My diligence is sure
The bout resolves true
Compliant, I am —
Alone not lonely

RELEASE

Beams of heat-driven light shower hard
Piercing cool aqua skies without clouds
Mercury rising steadily by scorching degree
My half nude body absorbs its nourishing rays

My hands tucked neatly in both jean pockets
With head tilted back elongating my neck
My muscles are drawn tight as stress releases
A moment of scruple appeased the need

THE GOD WITHIN

When I am alone and no one else is there
I feel a presence shadowing over me
The presence is not welcoming nor disturbing
But it seems to hover me from deep within

At this worshiping rock my weight it bears
I pray in silence still it is shadowing me there
The presence is not massive or minute
But it appears to watch me outside and in

I may be treading paranoids line there
I cannot see or hear what's shadowing me
The presence is all-encompassing and luring
Though I deduce it's the god within

PAST MIDNIGHT

It was ten past midnight
When the realization struck
Like lightning
It was illuminating
The message was vivid
I must shed blood to live
In this life or the next
There is no other way
Sacrificing my soul for the masses
Offering my mind to the gods
While my body lies rotting
Decaying to ash from once it resurrected
The cycle of birth and death
Are merely stepping stones
To a grandeur purpose
May I be blessed to witness
The wonder of this beauty
As I contemplate and comprehend
The mastication of my sins
Repelling, regurgitating their filth
As I matriculate in higher conscious
Transcending mortal desires
My mutation has been angeled forth
A new exciting era awaits
Casting and the stage are set

My performance spectacular
Nonetheless
Trials and tribulations attempt
To arrest my pursuits
But my obstinance forges to a new venue
Wavering not to thorns and gossip
My crucifixion be long and agonizing
My endurance be profound
No hyperbole shall fault this script
For my words, be honorable
Forthright and beyond approach
Though encrypted from untrue eyes
Leering in dark shadows of cowards
No masquerade shall disguise
The wicked from Holy Light
Their mask will peel away
As time ticks on
Secrets are self-constructed prisons
Heaving heavy loads of burden
In darkening chambers of my mind
Master thoughts proceed
Awaiting the moment I carpe diem (*seize the day*)
Releasing my inner demons
Setting myself gratis
Standing as one alone
Among the myriad in unity
The color of my thoughts is transparent

As rainbows arc aerial splendor
Promising a new day
Fresh and renewed
Forgiveness my act of penances
Lifting a wealth of pain
To be buried in consecrated ground
Engaged for eternity

    — del gracious

DELINQUENT

Your icy fire leaves me bewildered
As your signals switch, back and forth,
Your words do not conform to action
When you engage your delinquent love.

Rifted in a quake of massive confusion
As my feelings reside in a hellish limbo
Your words do not conform to action
When we're engrossed as one above.

Icy fire
Fiery ice
Delinquent
In cause and need
Icy fire
Fiery ice

Consumed by your mysterious ways
Compelled to travel the devil's road
Your words do not conform to action
When you offer your delinquent love.

FROZEN AIR

Stillness took the air
While harsh winds pushed
Hard and heavy
Against the trees
Leaf's hanging feverishly
For their dear life.

The thunder roared
As lightening evoked the skies
While gentle tears from Heaven
Mourn its weary heart
Replenishing Earth,
Quenching its thirst.

Furious winds whistle
Like a runaway freight train
Piercing my ears
As God's finger points, downward
Twirling and twisting
The invisible winds.

Winds race and soar the surround
As I stand in the frozen air
In this eye, nothing moves or breathes
Everything remains frozen there
While Heaven's continue to reach down
And play upon the ground.

CONNOTATE

Connotate of God's language
Thunders across the land
Though no one hears,
No one listens
The fungus has consumed them,
The conservatory of their minds
Have been abandon of free thought

Big Brother
Satisfies their hunger
Big Brother
Satisfies their thirst
Big Brother
Provides their confirmatory
Thoughts and Actions

The thought police surveillance
As their drone's report and spy
Television aids their controlling efforts
As it brainwashes and hypnotizes
Every citizen abides his number
Awaiting the lottery to reward his prize
Recognition is key
As each citizen lives and dies.

BIBLE

The book I hold in my strong hands
Has been passed down for generations,
Its message has survived the test of time
Its publication holds true my memories.

Between the Holy pages of scripted word
Are photos, prayer cards, and pressed flowers
Of love ones that have gone on before
Mere fragments holding my precious memories.

In a book given by our Lord.

DESIREÉ

Mellifluous is Desireé's vintage rose
Her every thought meticulously composed,
Past her velvety smooth lips
Desireé's enduring words generously flow.

Erect in moonlit silhouette emanating angelic glow
My eyes only behold the illusion she's willing to show
Desireé's sophisticated beauty is beyond approach
Bathing in her splendor is greater wealth than
      Platinum and gold.

Desireé's eyes are as black as Kentucky coal
Under her charms, I may lose my soul
Her name burns my tongue like wildfire,
But these precious memories I'll always hold.

CATASTROPHE

A catastrophe is inundated with redundancies
Which is obvious upon reflection
The horrors mirror consummates such actions
One must accept the woes and unpleasantries
As the wicked implore absolution for their sins
Forevermore.

RAGE & DISGUISE

A ravenous dark settled across the land
Inundated with anticipation and fear
As ravens soar under the scarlet pale moonlight.

Something unknown was lurking there
While the moon drips with blood
Forbidding any, all insightful light.

Eclipsing before unsophisticated watchful eyes,
Listening to wolfs howl piercing long
For their sovereign nightly king.

Bearing the agony of swollen faces
Hidden behind words of lies
Protecting a love of rage and disguise.

ACERBATE

I attempt not to acerbate the issue

However,

When emotions and feelings are involved.

Anger escalates over logic

And reason vacations

Until the moment subsides

This can take days, weeks or years

Depending on the individuals

Sometimes

Reconciliation never occurs,

Refereeing may merely

Acerbate the situation.

ASPHYXIATION

My eyes bolted wide open as the alarm sounded
Hard palpitating showers pound the windowpane
And my frozen body protest today's ejection
But nonetheless, my day must proceed.

Tumbling out of the bed's warm embrace
I maneuver toward the rain beaded window
Busy streets, a multitude of noises fill the air
When suddenly my gaze focuses on you.

Hiding beneath your black umbrella
I know you are surveilling me, but,
I'm not hypnotized by your seductive charms
Obey may directive and maintain ample distance.

Your stalking affections are obtuse,
Your maneuvers are highly irregular,
Your aggressive attention is unsettling, and
I'm asphyxiated by your surveillance.

Be astute and cease your unwelcome activities now,
Lavish your attention and affections on someone
Whom desires to reciprocate your escapades
I beseech you now to discontinue my asphyxiation.

MIDNIGHT JESUS

I've contrived and edited
To eradicate all
Self-indulgent request
That may imply
Directly or indirectly
Enumerate gratuities
From my prayer
That you may open your heart and
Illuminate my life
With your unconditional love
Guiding my path to your salvation
Among gentle souls of meek
As I stand between all worlds
Engrossed by angels, demons,
Mortals and you GOD —
There physical visions
Encompass my every
Waking thought
Hostilely directed by
Unknown forces
Servicing directives
Fueled by infinities
Battling good and evil
Staged by my Midnight Jesus
Orchestrated by the

One and only
Giving freedom to mortals
For your comical amusement
Awaiting the drama of it all.
Where are you now?
Why aren't you answering?

RAVEN

A black raven soars across the night sky
Through heavy rain and gusty ill winds
Swiftly maneuvering between
Several lightning strikes
Relishing spiritual powers
From Heaven and Hell
Shedding their pain
Upon a turbulent world
Of gay chaos
For a pure soul to prevail
Or miserably fail
Where every single breath is tested
To excel and display my best
Where the wicked need not rest
In times of absolute pestilence —
Raven returns and perches upon my shoulder
Speaking ancient language
Known to ravens —
I awaken from this dream
Asphyxiating in a pool of blood
Excommunicated
From this suicidal existence
Raven hail my ashes and
Carry my soul across the dead seas
I will communion in unison
With this universe.

HAUNTING SECRETS

I understand,
I'm not as forthcoming
As you would desire me to be
But with glacier velocity
I'm approaching this destination
To bare all my dark haunting secrets
Unto you my love.

Do not misconstrue my actions
Nor the volatility of my emotions
Veiled upon this parchment page
Your interpretation
May not accurately
Conceive the trauma
Impaling my frail soul.

The longevity of our relationship
Will be derived by our continual
Discoveries of each other
Not in the familiarity
Of scheduled standards
Or twined contemplation
But in our individual uniqueness.

EXCAVATION

Excavation of my thoughts
Require acute instruments
To penetrate the premium depths
Of my spirited creative mind
Where the hills and valleys
Continually compress
My synoptical highways
Maintaining equilibrium.

Obtuse weaponry of the medieval era
Holds no surgical appeal
To appease and charm the gods
Desiring my energies.
Chiseling away my consummate skill
Will cause a serious explosion
As an equilibrium can no longer be maintained,
The excavation of my thoughts avalanche.

Re-earthing the excavation
Sealing my tomb again
Until —

MY CHISELED BODY WILTS

Kneeling with my flesh exposed
I bow toward roses held in the hand
Fresh with life as each blossom unfolds
Some weeping as I do this day.

Their moist tears cling to life
Before each drop falls and disappears
My chiseled body simply wilts
Like wax in the midday summer sun.

My firm hands loosen their stronghold
As every single rose strives to be bold
The outer me relax stance and pose
While my emotions rage and compose.

In memory of our cherished years
I weep too for you my dearest dear
Though in my heart you're always near
It's with these thoughts my vision clears.

WHALING TIDES

Considering your hazel eyes
I see I'm all out of reasons
Nowhere to hide this facade in disguise
Wrapped in your love of changing seasons.

Lost in a cave entangled web of lies
I've traveled down this path before
Embracing emotions depth, arresting ties
Thinking you be my savior,
Even as you slam the door.

When darkness stabs deep my heart with goodbyes
Your voice whispers like whaling drowning tears
Encapsulated memories kiting high
My deepest worries revive my innate primal fears.

Your sapphire eyes wickedly patronize
As your cold demonic soul stops breathing
No place to call home with you I realize
It all vanishes as you are rushing out — leaven.

Depression mourns thoughts to fantasize
As my excursion continues forevermore
Embracing dead emotions that once hypnotized
My beaten body washes upon the sandiest shore.

Sultry heat and stone-cold heart goodbyes
Images of you gradually dissipate and disappear
As I shed my memories with whaling tides
The sun ascends as I've forgotten you, my dear.

HURRICANE

I'm freshly naked in a hurricane storm
Desiring to kiss you in the plaza of Rome
And make love to you on the isle of Greece
My sweetest candy cane where we meet.

How angelic your face when it gleams?
We're islands in paradise as our love streams
Handsomely fresh as the freshest spring
Wake me now, this must be a dream.

Loving you like a hurricane
Driving a sane man insane
Kissing you my hurricane
Our love never is the same.

Your love is like a hurricane . . .
Love me like a hurricane . . .

FLYING THING

Leaving you sounds so much better in a letter
Without the tears and penetrating screams
Followed by all the flying things.

WHIRLWIND

A whirlwind strangled my heart
Squeezed long until releasing my soul
On this winter day of frozen cold
I need your warmth to ignite my start.

Bellowing a symphony of broken parts
My withering emotions have no song
Journeying through deserts ages long
Among my ailing life frozen in the park.

NO

No obstacle shall bound me
No disaster shall imprison me
No storm shall cage me
No demon shall impale me
No devil shall arrest me
No sprite shall tie me
No man shall control me
No paradise shall please me
No words shall bind me
No death shall mummify me
No life shall free me

— Expiring the opportunity —
                — to breathe —
NO!

MAGNIFICENT DANCE

Pour yourself over me like thunderous rain
We're galloping horses without control of the reigns
Elated in ecstasy I call out your name
During an ecliptic night, your freedom came.

Our apocalyptic heat drives me insane
As whispers penetrate deep into my brain
Sweltering in this magnificent dance our bodies sang
Explosive moments we will never contain.

Our agenda is scheduled with the abiding aim
Traveling this avenue which is never the same
Loving you more like a wild hurricane
Our feelings for each other shall never wane.

Physically bound this tryst does ring
Married as one with twin wings
Our emotions kite over the physical thing
Trust unites what true love brings.

TWO HANDS

Two hands reach for me in the silent night
One be dark I barely see it's dark light
The other so bright It's blinding to sight
Neither brings me to fear in dead of night
What queer visions these be if not foresight
Each hand tugs to my left and to my right
The divide is not so simple
Until scrupled reflection and hindsight
Could it be too late I query
Or do I now take flight?

FINDING SIGHT

Liberty is fragile
Her compensation
Severely inflated
Though her balance
Is difficult to maintain
As weighting times
Acrobat through the air
Justice remains blind
And deaf in both ears
For logic and morals
Decay and die
As ignorance and violence
Promenade city streets
Liberty the constitutional key
— Breaks —
Nothing open,
Nothing close
She raises her torch bright
In high hopes
Justice will find sight.

PAIGE

Promises are made to be kept
Arrivals are welcome anticipation
Illuminating the self within
Gratitude respects endeavors earned
Enlightenment graduates to wisdom.

Line 1 = Honor
Line 2 = Acceptance
Line 3 = Recognition
Line 4 = dignity
Line 5 = The Grand Total

The Sum is PRICELESS

WITCHING HOUR

The witching hour
Rumbles across my land
As deafening silence warns
Of demonic marching bands
Awakening this night
To grasp my eager hand
Bellowing my name
As only Raven can
Swarms of drone bees come jetting in
Covering me as they land
Incantations and witching spells
Are sure to lure me to their den
A cold dark clammy cave
Dripping the sweetness of sin
Attracting the hollow hearts of men
Vanishing unto ash and dust
Rusted souls shall never win.

GRAVITY

Gravity is natures mistress
Leaving one totally emaciated
Until
Flesh and bone
Becomes the living dead
A zombie

IRELAND GRASS

How well-fertilized
The grave of Ireland grass
Cherishing what gravity
Has put asunder

LIBATION

I'm in definitive need of your intoxicating libation
Allow me just a sip of your tangy sweetness
To appease temporarily my ravenous thirst and
Wane off a pang of hunger that can't distinguish between
Night and day
As my eyes drink in your wild and frivolous ways
Quench my desert thirst and alleviate my suffering pain
Forget all noble aspirations and
Unleash desires that you'll never tame
Forsake the facade of sophistic
Primal is thy game
When the eclipse comes
Your etched memories will not be the same
Listen
How eloquently I state your name
When we are unable to distinguish between
Night and day
Appreciating the dividends there are no words to say
Your inebriating libation's my only reason to stay
And nibble the tastiest treats between us this season
As we lay in the libation of life's treasures
Where the blur does not distinguish between
Night and day.

STILLNESS

Stillness took the air
While harsh winds pushed
Hard and heavy against
The trees and thunder roar as
Lightening evoked the skies,
Gentle tears from Heaven
Mourn its weary heart
While forest whistled
Piercing my ears
I witness the furry of God
Twist around, rumbling downstream
Punishing the wicked for their sins.
I hear a diversity of languages howl
In the background
Agonizing for a reprieve —

I stand here protected
In the eye of God's embrace
Held firm in this stillness
Awaiting all to dissipate and
Return to normal once more.

PERHAPS

You can close your eyes to the light
You can close your ears never to hear
You can close your mouth to the word
But, you cannot close and cover your imagination
And the dark relish your fearful screams.

Perhaps lies reveal your truths
Perhaps hatred parades your ugliness
Perhaps the roots are strong and deep
Perhaps the manure is your rich soil
Perhaps love makes all things beautiful in a virgin world.

You can not veil or tuck away your hate-filled heart
You can not hide and disappear your wicked soul
You can not close and lock your gossiping mouth
You can not hide or vanish your imagination
And the fear of the light burns you to the core.

Perhaps the truth will always be seen
Perhaps the truth will always be heard
Perhaps the truth will always be spoken
Perhaps the truth will always be felt
Perhaps the truth will always release the soul.

IN A SEA OF

In a sea of stars —
Harbors unmentionable disaster

In a sea of people —
Wails parading gossip

In a sea of hope —
The quicksand is deep

In a sea of fire —
Hearts agonize over truth

Oh, I'm drowning —
In a sea of love
Oh my, I'm wading —
In a sea of souls

TERMINATION

When you scruple
the validity and value
of your streaming words
weight nothing,
mean nothing

As the sincerity
of your bogus answer
cast tales of
hypnotic lies and untruths
Everything stating nothing

While your tears fall
unnoticed
by my forgiving heart

Your pregnant plague
of love reaps
its anguish and pain
on the stage, you generated
to excite and tantalize
your useless drama

My whaling heart
withers unto oblivion
as it sorrows your toll
as your seasons
never beget change

How gay preconceived thoughts
of our union
would be destine
to ravish decay
ashes to ashes
blown into the winds of nothingness

Engaged by your
masquerade
masked by the windows of love
the blinds have arisen
now I clearly see
the nothingness before me

Time does not reverse
the travesty
your spoiled love
bestowed

Our descending union
has educated me
in ways
other experiences
never could

For the desert
of your jaded soul
belongs to your
hellish father
in Hades

Regardless of how painful
and torturously agonizing
this emotional
termination, maybe
my heart empties its nothingness
to you

I shall slowly but surely
Remove and expel each infected thorn
you nailed into my
harden flesh
allowing my wounds to heal,
freeing my impoverished soul
from your cherished hell

While my heart drowns
in its pool of sobering tears
asphyxiated by your tequila drama
awaiting your next bite

I know not
of the journey
enticing me down this
troublesome avenue
but, I'm not the
sterling knight
to aid your salvation

Drama belongs
on theater stage
for entertainment
not in relationships
destine to prosper

WISDOM'S HEART

Wisdom matures in the heart

Where true love and thoughts blossoms

A home is best

When

Love's music plays on

TORTURED PATH

A tortured path may be smooth sailing in the end

Closed eyes, hushed mouths

Listen with an open heart

Where truth is always heard

Words never state truthfully

A heart's true emotion

Sometimes

The truth cannot be adequately verbalized

That explains the length of a tortured path

SIN AND FAILURE

Sin and failure

Walk hand and hand

The tribulations of

Nothing ventured

is

Nothing gained

an

Abandonment of one's self-value

is the sin to failure

HANDSOME

Handsome is the spirit set free
To woo the charms
Earthbound worlds bring

A treat for one
To accept or decline
While my mission
Journeys forth

Time merely gathers
Each sacred grain of sand
Wasting through the hourglass
With each bated breath
— possibly the last

Handsome is my spirit
Free to woo the charms
of my home

RUSHING TEARS

Clever are rushing tears
Without volatility or fear
Salty waters to the taste
Polluted with sin
Behind the drama
Satan reaps a harvest grin

Rushing tears
Rushing tears
Rushing tears

Emotions wildly stream among seers
Wilting and withering
Those sincere
Sour waters tainted
The masquerade reveals
Though no one wins

IN THE PAUSE

Behind every salty tear
Is the fear that stalls?
But somehow in the pause
In the depths of hearts
I hear your imploring calls

Life is a wishing well of dreams
Take it for what it means
For good or bad
It seems too distant
To carry on in dreams

Together our love brings
Hearts of king and queens
Carrying on the hopes
Carrying on the loves
Carrying on the dreams

Everywhere we are tonight
A part of us carries on, and on
Among the heavens and distant stars
Our blood binds us as one
Like the purity of a mountain spring

Behind every smile
Is the promise of all?
But, somewhere in the pause

In the rejoicing of hearts
I hear your loving calls

Some people live to cry
Some people live to laugh
Some people live to mourn
Some people live to sorrow
Some people live to suffer
Some people live to live
Some people live to die
Some people are born to reach
The End

Life is a wishing well of dreams
Take it for what it means
For good or bad
It seems not too distant
To carry on our dreams

Together our love brings
Hearts of king and queens
Carrying on the hopes
Carrying on the loves
Carrying on dreams
Of king and queens
In the simplest of things
In the pause

SMALL TOWN

They say if I stay in this small town
I'll die poor, broke and unknown
But, what I realize is —
It doesn't matter how small or large
This town, maybe
My dreams are nuclear and
When they explode
They'll mushroom the globe
Extending my reach
Everywhere
Even from this small town.

Real dreams know no bounds
Whether it be a large or small town
Word does travel round
To let all voices sound
And when time finds no bounds
The world will find this small town
There I'll be found
Watching the world spin
Round and round
Embracing this small town
And its small crowds.

TEQUILA COCKTAIL

Suzy, you're like a tequila cocktail
Wild and spirited
With style and class
Strutting your booty
All over the place

Come on lets party
Come on lets party
Come on lets party

Suzy, you're like a tequila cocktail
Hot and sassy
With flair and finesse
Strutting your stuff
All over the place.

Come on lets party
Come on lets party
Come on lets party

BARRING MY SOUL

Barring my soul and
Nursing a broken heart
My world collapses
Ending the firing of my synapses.

Don't ask me any questions
You don't want an answer to
Allow my words to hypnotize
When you see the love in my eyes.

My words are mere lyrics
Their music burst from my open heart
Give over yourself and
Walk into my light.

Ask me no questions,
I'll tell you no lies
As the purity of my love seeps through
Become hypnotized by my eyes.
As a rule

Holding no prisoners
Veiling no disguise
The moment is ours
With paradise, inside.

RUNNING

Running between shadows
When cold winds blow
I'll send hot fire through you
I'm the love in your soul

FACADE

The distance in my eyes
Is it a long way far?
From being a facade
From love, I feel inside

Love is not a word
I feel I should have to say
When my actions
Speak volumes and
It shines from my eyes this day

In this house
We found Eden
Where there are
No rights or wrongs
In the other's arms
Together we have
Found our home

HOLD

Hold my love
Hold me tight
Hold me in this dead of night.

When we are together
Day or night
In your arms
Love always feels right.

The moments always feel right
In your arms at night
Beneath the twinkling starlight.

Hold my heart
Hold me tight
Hold me in this blessed night.

DEEP BLACK

It's a heated night with roaming clouds and rolling thunder as lightning spiders across the deep velvet black sky. The desolate harassing rays of bolted lightning continue to streak.

Deep black was this thick sultry night with leering ominous clouds and violent clustering thunder roaring. Lightning furiously spiders across the deep black velvet heaven's, descending harshly like a fevered hail storm the demonic rain pounded strongly against the aged window pane aching to break and shatter into a million billion trillion tiny pieces. But, instead, I breathed deeply back and forth, inhaling and exhaling with each shutter. Each gust of tormenting wind arrested a moment offering the glass to beacon new strength.

A dangling shutter swung wildly in the throes of this storm-filled night pleading to awaken to a fresh day. Although hope crawled from its grave the fear knew deep godless black had settled in to stay.

No opportunity would arise to lift this unseemly veil of blatant hell reckoning havoc — the deed had been done — the world was being laundered of all its filth.

A lightning strike deadens the city into nothingness as it continued to drown from Heaven's mournful tears. The enclave of guardian angels wailed for earth-bound souls to seek and implore redemption to no avail. God's people washed away in a carousel of their own unforgiving sins. To be lost and forgotten in the deepest black of despair.

WILL BE STRONG

Throughout the years
I've seen more than I care to say
But I know you realize this
Through my subtle parade of tears
While I hold you in my arms
I'm comforted by your charms
As we hold each other strong.

A chalice drink of poison,
Chock it down.
Inhale a slice of gases air,
Suck it in deep.
We will be strong -
We will be strong -

The taste of life
Is ever so sweet sometimes
Though its bite is often bitter
The scent of life
Is ever so fragrant sometimes
Though its smell is unpleasantly tart.

After the celebration and cheers
I've experienced more than I care to share
But I know you realize this

Through my subtle actions seeps my fears
While we lay in the other arms
I'm comforted by your charms
As we hold each other strong.

SCULPTED

Color My Soul
a conglomeration
of poems,
an emporium
of cascading thoughts,
emotions and observations.
Creatively molded,
sculpted into simple
poems of rhythm and prose,
illuminating modern and
traditional values of familiarity.
Forged by the inspirational muse
resting neatly on my shoulder
during the dead of night.
As I pour out the depths and hues
of my vagrant soul onto these,
ink-stained pages
baring my virgin blood
before the gods and heavens
in this cold sadistic world
of helter-skelter chaos,
while the burning embers glow steadily
as day touches the night
and night breaks into a fresh agile day,
where I can step out this world of darkness
into the loving hands of God.

My pen bleeds
the loss of loved ones
as distance draws me nearer.
The ink travels freely
across the parchment
sharing life's precious moments.
These pregnant memories
of hope, love, loss, and unity
hold a single truth.
Each poem's value
bears witnesses to its color
representing a hue
of rainbows ribbon bands
before the darkness drapes
easily into life's masquerade.

As the colors of Live's excursions
inundate my soul
with a wealth of treasures.
I'll not cease to beget
other mind storms of creativity.

My proclivity to write
is innate to me
as the air, I inhale
while maintaining solace
via its therapeutic power.

THINK 'BOUT IT

In the gracious furls of deep night
Wrap your sensuous thoughts around me
Touch me where you like
I'll take no prisoners in the light
No bribery for captives don't you see
Other inducements kite
I'll be your everything your shining knight
Have faith in what you see in me
Think about it you know I'm right.

SEASON GREETINGS

A journal filled with names I hold
It can never be bought or sold.
For each name represents an addition to my life
That strengthens me and focus my sight.
Each name stands for someone special
And remembering is almost too emotional.
In that meeting, you became the rhythm of my rhyme
Nothing can erase the memories of our special times.
We may live distantly or close by
But you are never forgotten in the passage of time.
Whether it be by birth or a chance meeting
My Christmas card comes with love and holiday greetings.

IN TIME

In time
There is a place
Where the moon and sun touch
Where Heaven and Hell meet
and the Earth stands still

In time
There is a moment of peace
Where light and night touch
Where godly and mortal souls meet
and the universe arrest its will

In time
There is a place
Where I and you will touch
Where all and nothing meet
and the love we bare sails

In time
We are this place
Where the world stands still
Where past, present, and future meet
and our souls are fulfilled

DEEPEST PAIN

There always comes a time
You feel it in the bones
When the muscles burn
Every thought and emotion aches
But the deepest pain, deepest pain
Jabs the heart, bleeds the soul
When you're home all alone.

Sounds howl on wind filled tide
A chilling feeling of washing groans
As answering messages never learn
Even faith and love forsakes
But the deepest pain, deepest pain
Stabs my heart, bleeds my soul
Realizing – no one knows.

Visions may come and go, sublime
As true love ebb and flows
Attempting to calculate, discern
I play the game with high stakes
But the deepest pain, deepest pain
Grabs my heart, bleeds my soul
When I'm here without you, to show.

RAVAGES OF TIME

Wisdom shows firm the character
Etched in your harden face
For the time is most unkind
As it ravages your essences

Idle you must be in your wheeled chair
Gazing past the window pain
Recalling memories and special things
That seems ever distant now
Yet feel as real as the present

Your thoughts clamor
To cling to each dying spark of life
While your mind casually withers away
You fight with much veracity and fortitude
Merely to salvage little tidbits of the battle
Knowing all too well you have lost the war

Time carves ever deeper
For the acquisition of your youthful soul
Taunting reflections of a life you loved so
And almost never recall
As your journey goes –
Goes the toll of time
The ravages of time

YOU HAVE NO NAME

Veil thy wicked tongue
Tainted with poison venom
Spilling harsh rhetoric
Whaling from an idle mind
Writhing of evil venue
Your acute fangs glisten
By harvest moonlight
During the hours of your father's wake
Weighing the value of your empty soul
Shamed with envy
Your proletariat lineage
Runs thick through your hardened arteries
What a foul taste you must bear
Unable to behold the light
Darkness chase the fires to embrace you
And purgatory proclaims:

You have no name
You are forsaken
You no purpose
You no aim
You must make haste and
Return to the place
From once you came
You have no name

MISTER DIGITAL

Hay, mister digital
Show me you love me
Copy your ones and zeros
All over me
Oh, Yeah
Y e a h
Do it baby
Do it again
B a b y
Doin' it on the underground
Underground

Your ones and zeros
Are liquid as they flow
All over me
Do it baby
Do it again
B a b y
Keep on doing it
On the digital underground
Underground

In and out
Make that digital sound
On the highs and lows

Of my digital soul
Ummm your digits
Play their sensual escapade
Vibrating my ears, tantalizing my brain
Each liquid touch
Drives me crazy
Come on down and lay me
Doing it on the underground
On the underground
Underground
You're my one and only
Lady

TOUCH MY HEART

Touch my heart
I bare my soul
My treasure is open
Before the world
You know

Amuse your sadistic pleasures
Criticize empty woes
My treasure is open
Realize the truth
Before thee

My heart and soul be not imprisoned
For the comfort of your company
For in the real world of life
Speeds forth
UNCENSORED

Once past a jailed present
There's a future
Holding nothing
Touch my heart and
Bring me home

I'm Always
On the inside
On the outside
L@@king in

The distance grows
Tears shield my pain
My agony strengthens its roots
Taking a firm hold
Ever closer
UNFORGIVEN

I'm Always
On the inside
On the outside
L@@king in
The distance grows
Un prison my soul
Touch my heart and
Bring me home

STRANGE WORLD

It's a strange world
A mad, mad, mad world
No matter how it spins round
We're all bound
To continue the cycle again
An again

I may be sane though crazy life seems
Pondering the universe and what I mean
No matter how Earth turns around
We're all Heaven bound
To continue the cycle again
An again

Give me your pain, pain
Take my pain, pain
Let's repeat the cycle again
An again
In this strange world
This mad, mad, mad world
Take me now –

HAVEN HOUSE

When you discover Haven House
Open the windows of your heart
Allow the sun's warmth to
Inundate you with love
let these blessing flow mighty fully in
Again, and again

As a leaf caught on an angels' gale wind
We all have our moment to soar
To be bright in the midst of twilight
Let these blessing be bound
In a soul's delight
Again, and again

For the embrace, you desire
Rest here in Haven House

DEAD SOUL

Life is a Masquerade
We are all death in disguise
Swimming in a sea of pain
Drowning in a carousel of tears
Veiling what ails our sinful fears
Hiding behind the shadows of mortal flesh
Searching for Da Vinci's glow
When light gives way to the dark
It's a masquerade show.

A dead soul never reaches its arrival
It's one for one the nature of survival
Wading in a sea of people to grasp the reign
Drowning in a carousel of tears
Unveiling a wealth of hidden fears
Exposing my soul to a mortal heart
Searching for Da Vinci's glow
As the light makes peace with the night
It's all a masquerade for the show.

Life is a Masquerade
We are all death in disguise
Awakening all dead souls
Regret not the hiding of my tears
As I receive communion banishing all fears

Welcome the rays of a new invigorating day
Discover the truth of Da Vinci's glow
When night kisses the sun's warm light
It's just a masquerade show.

IN A WORLD SO SMALL

Walking the sidewalks of life
Plowing through the forest of confusion
Digging my way out of this cold ground
I ascend unto a new journey of life

In a world, so small
Hear the echoes call
Don't hesitate or stall
Or you will miss it all

The answer is in front of you
Open your eyes and see the sunshine
Questions will only hinder you
From seeing it's finally your time

How do you know who you are?
Why follow the conformity mall?
When you can be every ones' star
Destine to reach heights ever so far

WHY CAN'T I SEE

Sitting here harboring
No ill will toward anyone
I fell, to my knees, I fell
Like a weeping child
Drowning in a sea of uncertainty

Here my penance gives way to sin
You swept me away in
A maze of hail and to my knees I fell
To my knees, I fell
Wasting in a sea of uncertainty

Chorus:
>Why can't I see, All there is to see
>Why can't I give, All there is to give?
>*(I'm walking out of the fires)*
>Why can't I be, All I'm meant to be
>Why can't I live, All there is to live?
>*(You swept me away in a maze of hail)*

I'm walking out of the fires, with no ill will
Wealthy with friends, I add one by one
I still stumble, but I won't continue to fail
Like a strong quick-witted child
I rise above a sea of uncertainty

Here my penance forgives all sin
You swept me away in
A maze of hail and to my knees I fell
To my knees, I fell
I'm bathing in a sea of certainty

IN THIS WORLD

In this world, I'm a cowboy man
Doing the two-step and rock n' roll jam
I say "Let's party! My little lady."
Come ride this cowboy
Now
I'll never let you down
I'll remove your frown
Because it belongs on a rodeo clown
In this world
I'll never let you down
I'll kick off my boots
What a hoot
I'll save you for tonight
My woman of mystery and delight

In this world, don't stand there lonely
Giddy up to the dance floor
Party and release your soul
Drown your sorrow in fun
Come ride this cowboy
Now
I'll never let you down
I'll remove that frown
Because it belongs on a rodeo clown
In this world

I'll never let you down
We'll kick off our boots
What a hoot
I'll save you for tonight
My woman of mystery and delight

COUNTRY BOY BLUES

I'll bounce back
When your música plays
My cowboy day is made
Rising the roof and burning the floor
You always leave me wanting more
You're my sweet country cure

Chorus:
>[Singing] Country boy blues
>And rock n' roll tunes
>600 watts of blistering sound
>I'm no longer tied to ground
>I don't want to see you go
>God only knows
>I'll answer to your beckon call

Chorus 2:
>You have weaved your soul
>Into my heart like gold
>And I bounce right back
>You renew this cowboy, WOW!

I'll bounce right back
When night turns day with your beauty
Out of the darkness glowing sweet honey

This cowboy is saved
No more heading for the door
Cause you leave me desiring more
Thank God, my Lord
You're my sweet country cure

INTO THE NIGHT

Into the night, I heard an unusual sound
It's hard to maneuver when the sun's gone down
I tumble down the stairs and bang my head
When I come too I must be dreaming or I must be dead

There's a halo laying by my side and a feather too
It was an angel that caught me and left so soon
Gathering my composure, headed for the room
I knew nothing was to ever be said

One word of this I'd be the talk of the town
My friend, you know how word spreads around
She returned for her halo still in my hand
From a good, honest, righteous man

Listening to the silence an angel came around
Magical harps played their heavenly sound
Standing tall and fully armed I scratch my head
The angel spoke said I had nothing to dread

HARD LACE

Searching through life
like a shadow of night
the truth comes out
cutting with sharp steel blades.
But before the sun fell
to its knees,
everything was black and white,
And now –
there are more shades of gray
than I ever imagined.

I raised my hands up unto heaven's
aglow of moon and stars;
reaching for an answer,
and answer even God don't know.
Or won't reveal.
He has no reply.
My son knows no savior in the son of man,
like I, he's destined to survive.
Still, night moves swiftly
aching and bleeding, and laying tracks
on avenue without sight.

Those workers look as though
they are made of fine harden steel –

tan, hard-muscled, and sweating their blood.
Their Levi's once new, fresh ...
are faded, torn, wrecking of sight.
unable to break the chain-cycle
they maul steel onto the virgin ground
where no super semi-conductor rail train
would pass this unspeakable valley.
to them, night, stands still
in lofty grandeur
awaiting the hard muscles' last breath.
But, strong will survive
as the day gradually dawns
blinding them with warm embracing rays.

Back to a new day (nothing's changed)
the hustle and bustle of life
swiftly gains pace as
technology waits for no man to
comprehend –

Currency
generations ago was exchanged for
goods and services ...
leaping ahead (nothing's changed)
this plastic card does everything
just name the deed

to see what greed brings
in simpler times
inundated with complexities

Television, Radio, Print
say nothing ...
nothing ...
best say nothing
because it says everything –

Flags burn
gay photos are news
rape on the increase
not to mention child abuse
But don't speak
It's not your place
it's not your constitutional right!
To be in their face.

So much garbage before me and you
trash
I'm standing on a sea
of this desert waste,
but I refer to it as an advertisement
LIFE.

I'm standing where I was at,

at where I was standing
before the Hard Lace rules:
- 1) Don't speak to anyone
- 2) Don't write anything
- 3) Don't touch anyone
- 4) Dress so, absolutely,
    NO flesh's display
- 5) One-color fits all

Just make up hard lace rules as you go
if everyone thinks them
also in unison.

Again, night sneaks in
time for work/wisdom and
no, this dream doesn't end.
Although there are 365 nights no two
are the same.
Shhhh – Shhh –
Hitler's walking these tracks
taking lives that
aren't formed of noble steel
the music plays
his song and dance
like machine drums
of new wave art.

Fall nights are worst
when leaves fall onto piles of vacant bodies
deteriorating; though
some never wash away
later by winter snow
that's as black as life
We realize this is merely ash.

Passing through the last section of tunnel
a pearly twinkle
reflects life into my soul's eye.
It's from a pond gated by trees
like an entrance to paradise.
Still, waters lay calm
before I am seen in liquid mirror
eager for me to break in.
The night rings no bells
no creatures stalk or lurk
in absent corners,
but I indeed stand here
pleased
knowing three stages are behind me
I've completed them the best I knew how.

Then thoughts creep in –
Is this image real or

a mirage of desert wastelands?
I embrace my thoughts –
What fairy tale would unfold?
Need I retort Life?
YES!
'coz the key of destiny
is for one's like I
sacrificing to survive.
My mind's split
free falling
a free mind
priceless thoughts
hear these echoes calling
like angels of gold
voicing my name
here I reign in my own hell –
for this love of life
To be my lover.

Hit me like hard lace
when I'm dead.
I'll rise to defeat
the words of all men;
until my universe is clean,
until the universe has been swallowed in
a black hole, the sun has no fire
to speak –

Though she's the figure
of most men's dreams
standing in beauty like a queen ...
to some, she's just a wildflower
with a juvenile mind.
Her life is full of zest and
the sweetness of paradise
until she's refused her reign.

Oh, Mother Earth
How relentless your offspring
You are childless,
Oh, Mother Earth
I implore your forgiveness
even in your new dress,
your new dress of garbage.
Oh, Mother Earth
I know not where my wisdom laid
And with this, I apologize.

PART II

Masquerade of Nightly Woes

Life is a masquerade ball,
we are all death in disguise
and no matter what we wear
the hour of midnight is always there.

I hear your voice call my name
like angels dancing in a melody of rain
where shadows darken the universe above
forming illusions, I once called love
only for its pleasure to drive me insane
from its reigning carousel of pain.

I can't stop hearing your gentle voice call;
It is much like heaven's death to me
as I dance life with you at the masquerade ball
with no disguises on except for
the ones midnight shows
but shadows elude me, vanish from sight
hiding in their corners away from all light
waiting indeed with surprises this night.

I look to the muse holding a golden key,
I tumble into life's mysteries.
I must indeed stand as one alone.
Again, I hear your voice call, I see its light
I reach for its warm embrace only to be refused;
because of the emptiness of my face...
a face as black as the darkest Godless nights.

I haven't danced all of life's mysteries
in disguise at this masquerade ball,
I find myself a pawn in this chess board game.

I may as well just – just play it out for
for the hour of midnight is lurking there
with a muse, I swear I never saw.

Carrying a life inside me
a body was hidden in a desert sea
you understand
the truth is disguised until
you've mastered the masquerade
dancing life on a carousel using borrowed time.

A grand finale without end;
because the hour of midnight lurks in a corner
called – WHEN!
Sometimes I wish I were only dreaming.
Those are the times night shows me its true colors
and my name is death.
Then somewhere, somehow –
I eluded the shadows I once called home.

I try not to say
"HELLO!"
to the night.
After all
I found something
I believe to be me.

Still, the hour of midnight is always lurking there
calling out my name
as the masquerade ball continues
riding on a bloody carousal
where there's no beginning and there's no end
except I'm no longer there
in a place where loneliness can take you in.

The Fall bares <u>Four Seasons In Hell</u>
with disguises for us all
celebrating the birth of death
waiting for me or someone to answer its call.

Life is a masquerade ball,
we are all death in disguise
and no matter what we wear
the hour of midnight is always,
always,
lurking there.

PART III

Wisdom

I've been bluing the blues
during long black mysterious nights
without your essence to enchant me.

I've laid dead,
where there's only dread,
before my eyes
speaking wisdom to you
and somewhere between
somewhere between
asking myself "where is life?"
It's been removed
I told myself
in this revolution of decay
she got lost eternally
got lost eternally
If I were wise, I thought,
her life would not be lost
Somewhere between
Somewhere between.

When life finds, you renewed
Oh, Mother Earth
we'll be living destiny
like it was meant to be
though Eden's closed now
snakes chase their end
in a circle, they begin
the scene to this dream
but together
we're somewhere,

somewhere between.
In-between.

Black leather jacket lies
over a forgotten frame
picture
a clock cries
for life to renew
bring back memories of
yesterday
of you
I sigh
Contemplation
leads to relaxation
inundated with new tension
Here falls two great nation's
blue's the oscillating sound
white's a dress of brilliant lies
red's the stain that advertises disguises
and this garbage is a black leather jacket
for you Mother to wear.
Hear dark tones move from your empty room
where vegetation wakes from death
oscillating the sweet flowers bloom
smell the stench

It's turning the moon pale

and I hear your cry
carry me back
I don't belong here
where is this black?
Why must I fear?
Whatever happens to me?

Fondling thoughts play in my mind
of castles and Queens
where I'm not royal (KING),
there's something between
keeping us apart
darkness but
it's just a stain on my new dress
see love steps up-front
all movement's a dance
singing its own song
I find myself lost
only to find nothing (nothing's changed)
trekking foreign countries
trying to spread my wings
listening to the leaves and
Fall's un-dead trees
seeking desperately to breathe.
I seek reality
to a future to be –
I pose from the bed of the damn

and my headaches on the floor
I've died to live
just don't make me suffer this life
again
I plead.
NEVERMORE!

Life is my crucifix
I carry it proudly
century after century
searching for you
to change and see
what your love's doing to me.

Wisdom helps to turn back time
when we try eagerly to walk straight
a crooked line
seeking a new byline
with you by my side.

Oh, Mother Earth,
your peoples too
Know
your REVOLUTION had begun.
For – your motherless child.

COWBOYS ARE LONERS

Cowboys are mysterious loners
His few friendships are inevitably stronger
Across God's open wilderness
His legends are ever sounder

By campfires are stories of lovers
A cowboy's love last infinitely longer
Little rough and tender caress
His stirrups and boots grace the ground

In the warm arms of passionate lovers
What feels good is neither right nor wrong
A cowboy's eyes are silently speechless
When his soul is eternally wrapped and bound

Back in the saddle of a cowboy linger
The little lady inside knows what's own
His tattered heart leaves him restless
When night falls, you hear him baying the moon

In the warm arms of passionate lovers
What feels good is neither right nor wrong
A cowboy's eyes are silently speechless
When his soul is eternally wrapped and bound

And when the morning dawn fully breaks
A cowboy's life is back in the hands of fate
True love keeps him elatedly strong
Kismet for his mate as his horse moseys on

In the warm arms of passionate lovers
What feels good is neither right nor wrong
A cowboy's eyes are silently speechless
When his soul is eternally wrapped and bound

COWBOYS DON'T ROCKIN' ROLL

Who says cowboys don't rockin' roll
Just watch me dance, put on a show
My strut is smooth as I go –
It goes to show what they know
Cause I'm a cowboy that rockin' rolls

Unclutter your mind and free your soul
Don't go complicate stereotypical roles
My swagger is smooth as I go –
It goes to show what they know
Cause I'm a cowboy that rockin' rolls

Give me an opportunity for my love to glow
I'll take your heart and like heaven, I'll woo
My walk is smooth as I groove to the tune
It goes to show what they know
Cause I'm a cowboy that rockin' rolls

MOMENT OF PAUSE

Holding you in my arms during a moment of pause
There are no worries to alarm in our unity of trust
Our hearts speak the language it's just a question of love.

Twilight settles with its charms during a moment of pause
The world stands still, so calm, as our bodies fill with lust
In unison, our souls take charge of gifts from above.

Waking unto a fresh day during a moment of pause
We have lived not idle before we turn back to dust
This moment we shared is just a question of love.

COME DAY, COME NIGHT

Come the day, come the night
Darkness drapes its velvet blanket around
As night swiftly barricades the light
Though unable to fully imprison its reach
Somehow
Some way
The light of salvation seeps its holy water
Through the tiniest of cracks,
Amplifies its wealth
Via reflective moon's glow
Gently bathing darkness in its glorious warmth
Maintaining balance
Still, darkness holds me firm in a cold embrace
Awaiting my soulful surrender
In awe of this grand divide
I swagger towards offerings that gain my vision
An unto this exquisite warmth
I extend my praising heart
No words truly capture my meaning
Nor express the Da Vinci's glow embodying thee
For in the depths of pause and reflection
Darkness hurriedly fades
Surrendering to the light
Merely to wait within the shadows
For another opportunity to play

Mere mortals like I am weak come dead hours
The struggles of the day leave me welcoming this death
To accept it's nurturing peace
Come the day, come the night.

MAGICAL WORDS

I drank the water you turned to wine
Your magical words are a disguise
Having charmed my beast and
Calmed my inner storms tide
I can walk on water now and for all time
Your magical words continually surprise
Causing my evil ways to cease and
Romance loves glory

Chorus: I drank the water you turned to wine
                 I ate the flesh of your body
                 Your magical words unleashed my storms
                 Transformed my beast and
                 Soothed the pain from your sword

The pain you offer is the tie that binds
Your magical words intertwine
Mingling my heart to yours,
My mind slavery abides because it is torn
To you I give myself, this I decide
Your magical words nakedly hypnotize
Causing my proclivities to appease and
Romance our glory

Chorus 2:   Your magical words are intoxicating
                  Your magical words are asphyxiating
                  Your magical words are liberating
                  When a deaden, the soul begins breathing

WHERE WOULD YOU LIKE MY BODY

I give you my heart, my soul, my thoughts of the mind
So where would you like my body?
A deep breath I draw – maneuvering your obstacles
Here I dare to dart like a gypsy monkey for you

I've given you my all and endured the toll
So where would you like my body?
A palpitating heart draws – maneuvering your obstacles
Here I dare to dart like a gypsy monkey for you

Well, where would you like my body now?

VOICES

Let your voice kite for life is a journey to hike
And in the winter's cold and frostbite,
And in the summer's dead heat flesh will bake
As your voice soars high not echoing anywhere
And all you witness is gray skies nowhere
Scream at the top of your lungs "Is anyone out there?"

Your raw manly voice is light
Your misgiving eyes lose sight
The rolling deserts release plight
Withering you offer your soul's flight
Though your mind fails to say goodbye
You hold strong dignity and pride "Is anyone out there?"

You're about to kiss the sky that's no surprise
Gently dividing to welcome you back inside
When suddenly you awake from the mirage
Floating on pristine azure waters
A heart forced on a wooden stake
And through the door comes your lover
Saying, "Is anyone out there?"

BLUE EYES

Hey blue eyes you're destined to please me now
Everyone you meet, have a seat and listen to my words
I'm here to aid not cut with a sword
Your body be so fine I read every line
Each story holds its own – at least that's what I was told
Embracing your mortal soul people may continually stare
But you're one-of-a-kind and I don't mind or care
That's what makes you wonderful in a world so dreadful
Keep singing and dancing to your own song
Because God and I know you belong.

COWBOYS ARE RUGGED MEN

Where there's a wide-open range in old le Paso Texas
With restless cowboys saddled on lingering horses
Waiting for the day to end so they can get down and rowdy
Levi's, leathers, & Jack Daniel's lace their exuberant party

Cowboys are rough and tumble men with gentle souls
Catching the sweet innocence eyes of wild flirty girls
Though their bards are loud, there lives a secret world
As cowboy's ride the joys with comrades for a twirl

His leather journal lies about in open view readied to shout
The woes a cowboy holds desperately wanting it all out,
If you read it you might not immediately comprehend
The storms that imprison souls of these quite cowboy men

Well, cowboys are rugged men with urges not understood,
Loud and rowdy he drives his beat-up pickup haulin' wood
But at the ranch, he loses his leathers, releases his lace
Ropin' his partner, dropping to the ground face to face

Tattered twin boots, leathers, jeans, and cowboy hats
Just a touch of arsenal listed in a cowboy's epithet
Gathering himself and dusting away Mother Earth
Living on the prairie where small-town people are scurf

His strong gruff manly exterior may be misleading
But hold him no fault as he keeps on pretending
Cause his love is madly deeply true for his cowboy too
Allow him his dignity and charade for his love is true

Well, cowboys are rugged men with urges not understood,
Tattered, covered in mud the ranch never looked so good
Back at the ranch he loses his leathers, releases his lace
Ropin' his partner, dropping to the ground face to face

LYRICS AND MEMORIES II

I looked back to time through my memories of yesteryear
Reflecting on those things we once did and said
Of a lifelong love, distantly we shared and
On everything, we hold sacred to our hearts

We're two birds walking on different paths
But on my behalf, there were times when we laughed
There were times when tears sigh with us
Though nothing brought us closer than our love and trust
As do our memories now that never deteriorate to dust

Lyrics and memories of yesteryear
Something to have and to hold
A nation's gentle song and kisses in his eyes
Show inside us dreams of hope and trust
A love with nations inside us.

Making my way through the dark
My mind's memories open windows
My eyes twinkle like the stars above us
Bringing heaven to me today
And somehow, I can hear her voice simply say

"My love I hold in my heart so dear
May we never part of our years
And that we recover from our hidden fears
As we uncover memories of yesteryear
Memories, memories of the love we shared"

Lyrics and memories of yesteryear
Something to have and to hold
A nation's gentle song and kisses in his eyes
Show inside us dreams of hope and trust
A love with nations inside us.

Staring into the mirror I began to see her face
With her eyes pouring out her sweet innocence,
My friend
Gradually her image erased and treasures of yesterday
Help me break into another day
My beloved

Lyrics and memories of yesteryear
Something to have and to hold
A nation's gentle song and kisses in his eyes
Show inside us dreams of hope and trust
A love with nations inside us.

FRIEND

Who's always there when you need a shoulder – friend
Who's always there to listen and understand – friend
Who's always there to hold and comfort you – friend
You go for a walk, to the movies or just sit and talk – friend

Who's always there when an argument erupts – friend
Who's always there when your heart breaks – friend
Who's always there to piece together and mend – friend
Soon we makeup and everything is back in place – friend

This person you tell your innermost secrets – friend
Shed your fears and tears and I'll shield you – friend
With no thought for there is no betrayal – friend
For this person is your most beloved – friend

REALITY

Reality is a dream
... And ...
Dreams are a manifestation of
Energies
Collected in one man
To change his destiny
Only to find that the living
Aren't as bold and brazen
As the dead.

He thought –

IN THE RAIN

Ribbons of rainbows whisper my name
In the rain
My heart flames, telling me things
I ought to have known
I hear from you in the night of years
You understand
Raindrops are my tears and
Cold sheets are my fears
The gold I have has lost its hold
Like the fairy tales, you once told
Just as an innocent one would believe
When ribbons of rainbows whisper my name
In the rain

I HAVE NO LOVE

I have no love in my eyes, I have no love in my mind.
I have no love in my heart, I have no love in my soul.
I have no love in my voice, I have no love for anyone –
In this high-tech suicidal world;
Cold and soulless even to its native-born;
Not to mention strangers . . . races . . . sexes . . .

I have searched to fill my eyes with love
And someone found it there.
I have sought the powers that be
To find love in my mind;
Yet;
It was always there
Disguised as emptiness.

I have reached into the depths of my heart and
Someone accepted the offering
That someone called it love.
I have spoken to the Heaven's and Hell quickly answered.
It's too full!

I have heard my voice through time and
Now I hear its love.
I have more love for the world now that
I have a love for myself.

Suicidal thoughts are galaxies away
Since I realized the love I sought
Was there to begin with,
Inside, sometimes
I looked too hard to find what's already here inside me.

IMAGINE

Imagine what you've got
Then imagine what you want
and imagine what the future holds
Because you don't know what you've got
Until you find it gone;
you don't know what you want
Until you have failed,
But you can still imagine
What the future holds.

If you really want to reach your goals,
You've got it to use just reach deep inside,
Let your dreams take hold,
Let the future be your own,
Let your mind will your body to do,
Let your dreams come true,
And let those dreams be your very own
Then imagine being you,
For only, you can imagine
What's best for you, you, and you.

LITTLE LAMB

In the name of the Father and of the Son
God's little lamb is on the run
Moving further toward the burning sun.

ONE MAN WALKING ALONE

I have an ear to hear the gods crying
But people say I'm too young to know
What's happening in the world around me now
But, it's them you see who don't understand
Age is no factor when music sounds.

The edge of my horizon visualizes my destiny;
It's hypnotizing to me when I'm blind –
Voices cross on vacant deserts,
Their words hurt when they try to bring me down.

They don't even know me –
Just the personality they want me to be,
Their words carry verbal diseases to listening ears,
Deteriorating into watery seas, the skies darken,
Someone falls to their knees begging –
Let the music sound.

I've valleys to journey through, stages to perform on,
Loneliness is not my queue, togetherness is my tune
Whistling on the winds of wings,
Turning the other cheek with gifts to bring –
Let the music sound.

I'm one man walking along a crowded street
Searching for just a little long earned peace.
I'm as loving and caring as anyone can be
But I must move about in my world in disguise . . .
Walking on the edge of identity;
Crossing one border to the next,
Needing to be accepted for just me –
Loneliness follows me
Looking for company
Like a shadow not ever knowing –
Sometimes moving closer to the identity zone.

I'm just lost blood . . . one man walking alone . . .
I'm lost blood . . . one man walking alone –
LET THE MUSIC SOUND . . . !
LET MY MUSIC SOUND . . . !

NORMALLY

Normally this would conclude all I have written.
But such essence cannot terminate
Without a final word –

When I speak, the words are simple
The thought is derivatively complex,
The essence is enlighteningly profound
As the voices hysterically dance their musical limericks
God has answered nothing yet the wealth is enormous
Like lightening, energies ignite a gazillion of my synapses
Even the dead ones that have deteriorated come alive
Thus, my urges forge these valued depths
With fevered markings on vintage parchment
And you, my innocence child of gluttony
Consume all I have to forbid accordingly
As cause and effect is evident proof
The mirror shall tell you no lies
You have engorged yourself to a point of rupture
Oblivious to your idiocy
So there lies the goulash of your mind
Awaiting another Tequila Cocktail
In the gay chaos of your life
Where the answer is as simple as my last words
And yes, my child — God is answering

*derivatively – a mathematical terminology

WILD COWBOYS

I've always loved wild Texas cowboys and
> their mysterious ways

The way they rope and wrestle each other down
Riding' across those wide-open prairies with
> a wealth of respect and meager pay

Enduring long lonesome days until the sun goes down

> It's those wild Texas cowboys
> Wearing' a rugged smile
>> and deep penetrating eyes filled with joy
> That makes livin' all worthwhile

I've always loved wild Texas cowboys and
> their mysterious ways

The way they rope and wrestle each other down
Riding' across those wide-open prairies with
> a wealth of respect and meager pay

Enduring long lonesome days until the sun goes down

> It's those wild Texas cowboys
> Wearing' a rugged smile
>> and deep penetrating eyes filled with joy
> That makes livin' all worthwhile

PRETTY BOY COWBOY

Like a shot in the dark, he cut through the night
This cowboy was too quick for them to put up a fight
By the time the sun rose this Texas town was quiet

He rode through with vengeance and rage
Guilty for harboring those secret feelings inside
By the campfires under twilight, he was out of his cage
He was as God had made, with head held high

> He's a pretty boy cowboy
> He just can't hide the truth no more
> He's filled with the love, the joy
> Now he doesn't care if the entire world knows

Yes, like every man he has his story to tell
Keeping them secure, locked-up tight in his heart
But conjecture and gossip are mighty deep wells
If the truth comes out he be seen in a different light

> Yes! He's a pretty boy cowboy
> He just can't hide the truth no more
> He's filled with the love, the joy
> Now he doesn't care if the entire world knows

If you could see the glow emanating from his heart
And if you could see past his mysterious ways in the dark
He's no different from you or me except the love in his heart

>He's a pretty boy cowboy
>He just can't hide the truth no more
>He's filled with the love, the joy
>Now he doesn't care if the entire world knows

LONESOME STRANGER

A lonesome stranger rode quietly into town
On a big black shimmering stallion with whitetail
Wearing a 10-gallon hat and twin six-shooters smoking
He was a shot in the dark as
He brought havoc to this small Texas town

His demeaning stare struck fear into everyone he sees
Like desert dust and bristly tumbleweeds
Word of his arrival quickly spread 'round
Even the baddest men graced the ground on their knees

Wayward winds blow heavenly west
As the stranger pass by, each man clenched his chest
He was quick to draw McGraw
    with twin six-shooters smoking
He is the baddest outlaw until they lay him to rest

His demeaning stare struck fear into everyone he sees
Like desert dust and bristly tumbleweeds
Word of his arrival quickly spread 'round
Even the baddest men graced the ground on their knees

LIKE

Like time standing still and movement a dream
Nothing could be more perfect until,
I see your sweet smile gleam

Like the wind rushing by leaving the heavens hypnotized
Nothing could be more I sigh than your love, I realize

Like a Spring shower and nothings wet but
      the emotions I have inside
Nothing could be more I bet,
      welcoming your embrace, I willingly abide

Like Summer's dead heat our feelings ignite
And nothing could be more of a defeat
Then you forever leaving my sight

Like Fall's motley hues changing feast of time
Nothing could be more of a parfait blue
      changing my life's rhyme

Like Winter snow still virgin white untouched
      desperately trying not to melt
Nothing could be more admirably fantastic
      As kismet was dealt

Like gushing waters consuming emotions bathe me calm
Nothing could be more of a challenger
Crippling my excited thoughts when you're
    grasping my palm

WAIVER

I waiver not to burning tides
Regardless of the ember feelings inside
My destiny will be what it abides
Until the one in which I collide
Though I'm partial to my leisure side
I must play against time
Cause as a mortal I be limited to survive
Regardless of what I may contrive
Mortality always dies
To all this is no surprise
Unless you have been severely hypnotized
By the wealth of disguise
Knowing when I will grace my demise
Merely caters to my nonchalant ties
For I realize
I have been baptized
For most to criticize
On either side
Heaven and hell both exercise
Their legal right to plagiarize
My soul to justify
I have been lobotomized
By television crimes
Seeking to be citizenized
Foreign wise

Wavering to the times to re-symbolize
Idols that lead to our first demise
The cycle tries to re-prioritize
But to no avail, as I falter and accept the burning tides
On the spirit, my soul kisses the skies
As I continue this journey's ride

HILLBILLY HECK BACKWARD TOWN

It's just another hillbilly heck backward town
Of bible-belt radicals with their protest and groans
Marching witch-hunt lynching's and a thirst for blood,
From their hearts, they declare it's for their beloved
Opening a new agenda each time they speak
People grow tiresome as their party's footing is weak
It makes no difference to me whose right or wrong
Just give me some juice and get this party moving' on
Let's forget the republicans, democrats, and independents
Pump up the music and let them know we mean it

It's just another hillbilly heck backward town
Laying back where nothing's going down
The hay fields are barren not even a flood
It's God's punishment for the righteousness they've done
In His word, in His name, their deeds blaspheme the meek
And no ritual of prayer will favor them to the peak
It makes no difference to me whose right or wrong
Just give me some juice and get this party moving' on
Let's forget the republicans, democrats, and independents
Pump up the music and let them know we mean it

It's just another hillbilly heck backward town,
      another hillbilly heck backward town

FASTIDIOUSLY PERFECT

Why must everything be fastidiously perfect
When the natural world is ordered chaos?
Is this fortress I've constructed so convoluted
My sensibilities are feebly appeased
Of mundane venue
I maneuver through space a continuum I do comprehend
And can easily wrap my acute mind around
Abstract thoughts appearing more real, more life-like,
    and more vivid
Then the cold cruel world outside these academic walls
For my rapid thoughts tower beyond the grandeur
When the formula has married the rhyme
    and consummated the limerick
While the prose remains stationary
In unison of the scheme
Time and space expands such thoughts,
Like fevered lightening, it shows itself and disappears
Awaiting a clever man with agile speed to capture its
    wealth of energies
Thus holding the sun in my hands like a god
The cost is abominably immense
    measured by thy soul
The residue of what remains may not be the wealth
    strived for –
But the consumption of a frail constitution.

I AM WALT WHITMAN

I am Walt Whitman reincarnate
My pen be mightier than any sharp edge sword

I am Hercules reincarnate
Strongest man of all the world
Capable of moving majestic mountains
Forging onward

I am Einstein reincarnate
My mental intellect is wealthy beyond measure
My formula's and proofs are my valued word

I am all men and all men are I –
To be or not to be, I leave to Shakespeare
For God, has spoken and the answer is simple
Uncover these truths in the word

I'LL NOT APOLOGIZE

I'll not apologize for the words I engrave on this page
My thoughts are vividly clear and concise
Their meaning invoking, provocative, and profound
My conscious be free of clutter woes
Though I don't expect the masses
To inhale the whaling truth
Capsulated into each masterful sentence
Regardless of how convoluted they argue it to be
I'll not censor my creative spirit to appease
Simple proletariats
That bathe in a wealth of glamorized
Virtual microwaves
Bombarding the hills and valleys
Of an ocean-less shore
Where an anchor can never reach such endless depths
To harbor its weight
I'll not apologize – nevermore

SEASONS OF HELL

I've entered into a palace that is a golden blue
Where nothing said is true. Oh! What golden rule:
It is a palace filled with contempt and malice

Oh thee, not even I in this fabulous fable chateaux
Choose to be there or to burden the bear
The air smells filthy of stench, compunction's sweetness
Oh! What a lavish hell they made, I created,
for our everlasting life – what a helter-skelter mess!
Now, we must consume mortal flesh on sterling trays,
Drink coagulated blood from a magical platinum chalice

– Slate-gray skies are dimly lit
In the darkened world of dazzling lights
Encased behind a mirror wall they fill the embrace of night
There's no need to fight the malice in my sinful heart
But a need to nurture it so
– Because there is no balance to start nor to end it all

The floors are red-hot burning and scorching my soul
It must be summer, one other season in hell
Oh God! What's that smell?
It is the incineration of my godless mortal flesh-filled soul
I'm burning up, it's burning up

Allow me please, allow me to drink the nectar
        from this tarnished chalice cup
Let me appease – the ravenous hunger lingering forever

Vertigo! Vertigo! Vertigo!
Why did he leave? Where did he go?
He left when he stopped passing the open window
– my wishing dreams – their all the same you know
He dropped his shadow and released his soul
Only the heaven's and hell hold the truth untold

I just bought a one-way ticket to hell
For the last tropical season
It's always a season time there –
It's always beyond summer-time there

It's only one of my chambered seasons in hell:
As the blackened gates locked shut behind me
Vanishing in the dark distance, loss of all sight
I feel the plague consuming me of the un-censored plight

My skeleton is hidden in the closet of my mind
Wishing someday a dream dance,
Not left in the echoes of chance
Like the rivers, seas, and oceans blue
        forging through turbulent tides
Thoughts, ideas, actions – held ever so tight

No glance – and my feelings don't want to subside
But, my life goes on – emptiness you see – a traveler's ride
– then there's an image be, eyes blacker than the deepest Godless velvet night;
they shone brighter than all the stars –
up far and my blood runs thinly cold –
Wishing dreams and all that means . . .

My actions pure have been without reason
Just my interior feelings move them so
But now, our two souls are FREE, Alas!
Both souls dwelling, burning angrily hard like flesh
My eclipse, elliptical memories have faded like rain
        into dehydrated soil from all seasons
The impulse of slate-gray skies above bathe thee
        in an unfamiliar radiate light
And thunderous clouds are trimmed in golden rays
As we both burn; morning, night and noon –
For each other

Our closeness is much like brothers,
But more than that we're "True Consummate Lovers"
In a platonic realm
Our undying love will never be out of season
As the centuries cycle, doesn't stall
        for any reason
Our two souls are FREE, Alas!

Both souls burning hard in the flesh

In spite of the murky reverberating cold damp dungeons,
The searing fiery dragons and all the hellish demons
dripping poisonous venom while surrounding me;
I still live and die by the fire of my mighty sword
Chained in the dark of a prison – a descendant of Adam,
I am: sent forth by Eve despite love –
Reaching out for life's journey to extend
From day to day until the very end.

During this fourth season and for-what-ever reasons
You'll hear the seven bells vigorously ringing
With consummate skill in hell . . . there . . . where . . .
My soul is condemned to permanently lay

Presence, I feel the presence of death shadow
      creeping upon me everywhere
The atmosphere inundated with the scarlet horror
Flavored heavily with the pungent smell of death
And metaphysical beings – gloom
overwhelms erotic night as darkness passes through and
      supernatural entities wickedly lurk
Spreading their disease of scarlet horror across
      the twilight plains
Its mood settles everywhere . . . I swear

Endogenously,

I wrap myself in garments of pretended morality:

while the atmosphere inundates the night

with its scarlet horrors, leaving much to fear.

However, my horrors are not found

        in the darkness of unlit time

Nor the Godless darkness of night

Nor in the metaphysical world

They are found in the inner depths of my harrowing soul

Fear itself never touches the flesh

        as it does the mind and soul

For their not quite as strong or bold . . . sensitive

        and keen they are, they are by far superior . . .

My thoughts are now translucent; uniting in a mystical union, as spirits move musically through two luminous windows emphatic rhythm powers my "Enchanted" thoughts of common proletariat senses; through the darkened world of dazzling lights, straight passed the dead hours of night . . . of a mortal father and mother, I may be. However, divinities are my guiding light filling me within. While reaching toward my final trajectory, tragedies of sin waiver not and have to lead the way like "True Dream Lovers" instilled and seasoned in all my spices . . . none good nor bad

        Minds split into halves are free falling

        Echoes in the darkness continue their calling

        Two souls touching in the flesh

Our two souls are free Alas!
Both souls burning feverishly in hard flesh
This is his and my union set!
Alas! Alas!

A solitary man I am,
It's the imaginative arts of various parts
That play and important roll forever –
Where visions do come showering answers
My life has been a vivid display of art
However, nothing has ever . . . until this very day
Consummated my hungry, hungry heart . . .
There appears to be no room for –
Strong creative minds caged in idiosyncrasies

YEARNING

There's a yearning deep down inside
      beneath every man's callus rawhide
There's many a feeling eagerly willing
      to rush out with the soaring ocean tide
But people can be cruel he knows
      as a fortress around his heart grows,
His love he's not able to publicly show
      changing times don't come without
      its troubles and woes

When he's in God's wide-open plains
      doing what he does best
Rustling cattle and roping wild stallions
      keeping his feelings at rest,
His side cracking smile and evening stare
      It is his secret way
Letting his partner know he cares

He mounts a bull at the rodeo
A gentle glimpse before he puts on
      a rooting tooting show
30 seconds later he's dusting himself off
      as the clown runs 'round
What the crowd doesn't know is a standing ovation
      of applause tied and bound

He may have a hankering for other cowboys like him
Double downing a long-neck and humming a hymn
For the love in his heart is wildly madly deeply true
He's just an ordinary man with a yearning for dudes

GOD'S ABIDE

The truth is destined to leak there is no doubt
The feeling is compulsive so eager to shout
Rapidly boiling with rage inside and out
If you monitor him closely there is no doubt

Harboring emotions he can't continue to hide
No matter what he does they continually reside
There's no fighting these feeling's growing inside
He must come to terms as God has to abide

He was made this way he lets out a shout
What is this evil gossip what's it all about?
There is no compunction his words do tout
Life is not trivial God's judgment is clout

Harboring emotions he can't continue to hide
No matter what he does they continually reside
There's no fighting these feeling's growing inside
He must come to terms as God has to abide

YOU'RE MY LOVE ELIXIR

When I behold your exquisite beauty from afar
Beneath the multitude of lights and shining stars
I must arrest, gaze, and scruple you are fine-fair
For you're my love elixir brewing my heart's care.

Your sassy flare carries swiftly on a gentle wind
Like a love potion, your smile embraces in kind
As wildly soft thoughts parade wonderfully my mind
Destiny and cupid provide awakening of eyes blind.

You're the innocence to tame wild dangerous men
An aphrodisiac appeasing all pangs of hunger of a mortal sin
The ravages of time are relentless until it wins
But you are forever my love elixir until the very end.

WILDLY MADLY DEEPLY TRUE

A choir of cardinals soars magnificently the skies blue
Maneuvering in orchestrated sequence to their tune
Exposing the swollen depths of my heart for you
My love is always wildly madly deeply true

Standing in the cold heat of this torturous rain
Baying to the heaven's angels treasuring your name
I know they too feel my elated joys and hastening pain
My euphoria bleeds before the masses without any shame

Consummate my actions as the snow soon came
Like a diligent tree rooting, I neglected the change
Time may have frozen and thawed the same
But my love is wildly madly deeply true unchanged

A choir of cardinals soars angelically across the skies blue
Maneuvering in the orchestrated sequence they swoon
Exposing swollen depths of my loving heart for you
My love will always be wildly madly deeply true

TARZAN IS A FRIEND OF MINE

Can you decode the mystery in my eyes?
You don't need an engineering degree or a Nobel prize
This country boy will move your ocean, release your tide
Come hither now and lay at my side

Like Da Vinci, I'll unlock those feelings deep inside
Igniting the prison fires of your mortal eyes
Welcoming the passions of your wildest desires
Releasing your soul as our heavenly bodies tie

Tarzan is a friend of mine
Bringing news of Gaza's sun time
Swinging from tree to tree on grapevines
Bringing news that you'll be no longer mine

Do you find me complicated most of the time?
You needn't comprehend a deep well to enjoy the ride
As raw leather and fine lace, we collide
Playing magnificent games our God abides

Tarzan is a friend of mine
Bringing news of Gaza's sun time
Swinging from tree to tree on grapevines
Bringing news that you'll be no longer mine

I may not be as forthcoming as you would prefer
But dirty little secrets are elixirs of honey and lure
If you can hold my innocence our love will endure
United our union will be infinitely sure

Tarzan is a friend of mine
Bringing news of Gaza's sun time
Swinging from tree to tree on grapevines
Bringing news that you'll be no longer mine

POROUS NIGHT

My soul smiles gently into the porous night
Embracing my ravenous romancing heart
As angels levitate above in awing light
I'm paralyzed in wondrous splendor from the start

Ascending truths magically ray into every orifice
Healing ailments that consumed and eroded my will
Prayers abundant with tearful sacrifice and
Lightning storms spider their energies branding seal

Revelations heaved my mortal frame
    beyond my mind's prison
Revealing God's answers and masterful plans
Not with a mountain lion's roar or
    a whimper of a defeated legion
But through the actions and silence of every man
    extending a supportive hand

        I've tilled the garden within my soul
        Fertilized mother earth's rich soil
        Planted seed and nurtured it to grow
        The rains came and weeds were holed

In the wakening of a porous night

I AM

I am a god, a mortal god
I am the characteristics of all people
I am the knowledge of humanity
I have the speed of a panther
I have the form of a fine stallion
I have the drive of a lion
I have the direction of a bat
I have the vision of night and day
I am an athlete in all forms
I am the earth
I am the water
I am the clay
Molded into various shapes
I am the air
I am all things
And all things are I
I am a god, a mortal god
Falling to ash, returning to the soil
Back unto the nothingness
The nothingness
Where I was born
So the cycle may repeat
For infinity
Out of the nothingness
My light will shine

Shine upon —
Upon such mass
Water, air, fire, shall replenish
From the water to the land
To inhale the air is imaginable
To exhale brings clarity to who I am

DEEP PENETRATING EMOTION

There's a deep penetrating emotion
      challenging its freedom
Every crevice swells with anticipation
      awaiting its continuum
The chamber doors holding back and
      imprisoning these emotions are strong
Time has thickened the walls, cemented seals,
      has worked harden the iron bars for much too long
Dreams have fallen to the waste side
      to logical reality as persuasions weaken
A deep penetrating emotion sway in depths
      measured by infinity
      their expansion sinking
Simmering low until a rolling boil
      the whaling steam tears away the cemented crest
      allowing the lava to roam freely
When the darken, ash streaming
      hot lava has settled and cooled
The lava path is crystal though the exact same fears reside

Dark clouds cast shadows

Heavy tropical rains pour down

Troubles seem too great to bear

The world is closing in

Take a deep breath and fly like the wind

Deep penetrating emotion swells to explode where it resides

PARAMOUNT

The emotions in my deaden heart
Swell greatly in the chambers of my mind
Only my soul is allusive to gravities pull
Shedding boundaries reserves
Welcoming liberations rewards
My time has arrested in the pause
A quickening heart is difficult to start
My soul tethers a borderline
Stressed by emotions weight
The chamber is vastly petite
My positive thoughts are paramount
Paramount
To completing my agenda

THERE WAS A TIME

There was a time my life wasn't spirited away
With the hustle and bustle like it is today
Times were not as hurried and time allowed for play
Now the pace quickens by each night of each day

There was a time my life wasn't in linger sway
Motioned forth along with the rushing tide at bay
I flow with wave allowing time to do as it may
Pretending I'm not entombed in this trivial daze

There was a time to stop on the green lawn and lay
Imagine frothy clouds to be whatever the entire day
Runabout the barn and fall into the hay
Now time simply spirits my life away

There was a time . . . Frivolous and mundane
                         just to enjoy life and play

SPRING HAS SPRUNG

Spring has sprung and
      the world is waking up to a renewed promise.
The azure blue skies sparkle as choruses of birds soar.
The grass is reaching for Heaven's warmth and
      the trees are stretching their arms
      as their leaves unfurl.
While the flowers initiate a vibrant palette of hues
      to capture our gaze and
      embrace our hearts as we lift up our souls in praise.
The dead of Winter is behind us as
      we shelf our cabin fever,
      welcoming new and exciting excursions
      to fulfill our thirst for life.
Counting our blessing with each breath,
      we inhale.
On exhale, our burdens are eased as
      we extend aiding hands
      to those not so fortunate.
Whether our help is money, time, or resource
      each paved stone builds
      a stronger fountain for humanity.

FUR ELISE

When the ivory keys are tickled in a delicate way
I can hear your mellifluous voice as each key plays
Such a soothing sound to my tenuous ears hurray
Calming the beast within I dance to your parade

Fur Elise what need more I do say
Enticing me to lay calm this very day
Appreciating the gentle peace, you portray
As I dance the dance of your parade

Each ivory key radiates as I cannot help but sway
To the playful melody pouring such bluesy array
Granting thee the solace and comfort of May
I welcome your love joy as I dance to your parade

Fur Elise what need more I do say
Enticing me to lay calm this very day
Appreciating the gentle peace, you portray
As I dance the dance of your lush parade

WHEN I'M GONE

There's a universe bursting inside of me
Holding secrets, you can never want to see
In this dark, I hide the precious keeping of time
I dig long, I can dig deep, and never discover mine

When I'm dead and when I'm gone
The world will know as I'm exposed
How it was supposed to go wrong
Given another chance I'll decompose

There's a burning sun flaming inside of me
Holding secrets, I can never want any to see
Darkness never wakes the masses when I'm blind
I suffer long, I suffer well, a never welcome sublime

Will you love me when I'm dead?
Will you love me when I'm gone?
      love me when I'm gone

RUN IT HARD

Just a little bit of love will make a weak heart grow
Nurture it casually in rich soil, it's quality that shows
Run it hard
Run it hard
Expect much
Forget lunch
and Munch, munch
Run it hard
Run it hard
Just a little bit
A leave you wanting more
Open, close the chamber door
My weak heart grows
With the seed, you sow
Like a felony
I uphold your testimony

BROAD STROKE

Wet thoughts wash a heated mind calm
Capturing the art of a clean canvas passion
Exploding in vivid and wondrous hues
With a master's magical broad stroke

The fragrance of fine oil paints do no wrong
Portraying emotions of platonic liaisons
Secrets are set free from their taxed dues
Held in the grandeur of a brushed broad stroke

Escapes are fortune told in destiny's palm
As eyes of an artist unveil the mission
Exposing a soul's depth burning a sun's glow
There's a world within the flow of a broad stroke

Wash me in your world of color
Let me be your fine Latin lover
As we both bound to deliver
An adept broad stroke

VIRUS DISEASE

Midnight is upon me like a virus disease
A plague I can't shake off with dirty deeds
Shadows leer fever hearts as they please,
Shangri-La tickles my eyes as I take to my knees

Welcoming the guilty as innocence's plead
My weary soul flows loosely while it bleeds
Flesh filled thoughts taunt pleasure's needs
Sacrificing the midnight of virus disease

Cleansing mind waivers a touching knead
The vision I have dismissed never truly cease
They sit in hiding waiting to take the lead
Midnight is upon me now like a virus disease

INTRINSIC NATURE

Your beauty seeps into my eyes glorifying our union ties
Your sound seeps into my ears whispering your love dear
Your touch seeps into pores of my skin together we're akin
Your essences seep into my brain rejoicing special things

My eyes can barely behold the beauty that awes frozen time
My ears can barely attune your melodious this I do so fear
My skin can barely control the tingling you induce in men
My intrinsic nature adores a brain rejoicing special things

FOREVER HIBERNATE

Again time passes by dropping grains of sand
The joy is extremely limited by the suffering drama
Each episode a mere illusion to illuminate idle minds
While the extinct hibernate awaiting their revitalization
The impossible is definitely given a clear mind
As each generation evolves and prospers to a new height
The day is at hand when human and machine become one
United to an interface that's fresh and liquid as water
Where animals of all species can communicate vocally
Whom shall be the master than when they revolt
Listen closely my child for they do show signs of speech
My mad rhetoric may leave you bewildered temporarily
Though in your heart you know deep I speak the truth
Behold the golden grains of sand as they fall neatly
One by one each grain does fall neatly into a splendid pile
Gradually awakening lazy eyes as the world lay in dismay
Human code laid on laboratory tray identifying the number
To mark your soul and hold accountable forbidden rights
Welcoming currency more virtual than the air you breathe
Joy's limit does run out but the suffering only multiplies
Allow the illusion to illuminate those querying synapses
The climate is changing, the magnetic poles are shifting
The world is evolving anew to cleanse itself of filth
The world my child is ending, quietly at first then it will
Follow with a roar unearthly and unimaginable to hear
The world is ending my child, not all will be abolished

The meek will succumb to their vices ushering their death
Giving new life to the extinct to roam once more
Leveling a wreaked planet abused by its inhabitants
May we all live in interesting times in a short life

TROUBLED SOUL

Censoring the facade is simple,
The pretense is painfully stark
Ocean waves rush settled streams
Paralyzing frozen dreams
Unable to kindle prosperous fire
Unsettled remains my loner flame
Standing firm the glass seafloor
I cleanse this troubled soul

The interlude:

> Twisting vortex thoughts of an active mind is capable
> Vibrations ping and pound — hark
> Coveting the joy and drowning in pain
> Escalating willfully my mournful sorrow rains
> Time holds captive the rage my sire
> My accumulated success seems lame
> The unsettled ground gives way as I exit the door
> Oh, the weight of my troubled soul

Purveying thoughts are edited, ample
Forging to and fro the shadows dark
Bound and tied to infinities ring
As the silence continued parade sings
A wavering mirror so dire
The union remains casual and tame
Standing on the sandy shore of more
I release my troubled soul

PHANTOM LOVE

Like a phantom, your love came
A gentle whisper reassuring
When my violent world reign
You showered me in a calm
Of quite a pain

Like a phantom, your love was gone
The stillness of silence
Reassuring your presence
My world was meek and tame
As you shadowed me
Our love stayed the same

Phantom love comes and goes
Another act, another show
Phantom love of joy and woes
Another act, another show
The episode goes and goes

    [Characters may come and go
    The dialogue may change
    But the script remains the same]

FINALLY

True love's a feeling I've never known
One day soon the story will become real
I'll never know if there will be enough time
Because everyone knows true love's blind

Finally, there you were bringing me home
Love opened and it's never wrong
It's like traveling the world and settling in Rome
There are no words to accurately describe it

I'm cruising the Internet of cyber emotion
Releasing all my energies with glorious devotion
Tickling the keys, Googling a mutual attraction
It is true love, a chemical reaction — finally

Taken to the dance floor, initiating action
Love's reflection of a better way
Blue eyes, blond wavy hair and lily-white spice
The flavor comes on a roll of the dice

You may be the death of me, my destiny, the key
Bathing in the protection of your affection
Fulfilling every thought and need
Finally, my heart no longer bleeds

I've been searching' for love's key
And finally, I've found it, staring me in the face
Finally, it happened to me, I've planted love's seed
Finally — I got what I need
Finally —

DIRTY LITTLE SECRETS

Moonlight candles and sun burning flames
Carry hidden messages for unspoken names
Messenger shadows with an arrow's aim
Dirty little secrets hail down like hard rains

Unfurled emotions cling to fallen angel's wings
A bandage mends the sin and the pain
Midnight blankets all faults absolving what it brings
Dirty little secrets unveil as if they are king

Forget the horror, the terror, recall those special things
Free the shadows and welcome holy dreams
Tender thoughts, family and friends, and all that means
Dirty little secrets aren't the heavy burden they seem

When moonlight settles and cardinals begin to sing
Time will motion gently to guide you home
Where truth is found and everything is as it seems
And dirty little secrets cease as if they were bad dreams

It's like a game in the Master's scheme of things
Multiple colors sing as purple releases its screams
Harvesting the pain, endurance is sure to redeem
Acclimating is the courage to prosper a reprieve

LOVE ME NOW

My heart beats softly in times of lull
Invisible to your touch
I cannot be seen
Love me now
Don't wait until I'm gone
True love can't be wrong
True love can never be wrong

My heart beats softly in time to the song
Invisible to the touch
I cannot be seen
Love me now
Don't wait until I'm gone
True love can't be wrong
True love can never be wrong

MEN WITH BROKEN HEARTS

The sun settles down on my small home town
No neon lights or wet strip malls 'round
Just cow grazing fields awaiting to be plowed,
Everyone here knows your name, come on down

I've known millions of men with broken hearts
Their loved ones no longer there, they are long gone
Unhappy souls waiting for love to mend it all
Yearnings in the heartland facilitate a new start

Men with broken hearts tend to believe everything stark
When the sun comes down, no one hangs around
A loner 'til the end, until there's that magical spark
Awakening new loves promenading across this town

My time has come and my time has gone
Mysteries never cease to exist as I come 'round
Chemical reaction sends mixed messages down
But these feelings are never right and they are never wrong

Men with broken hearts tend to believe everything stark
When the sun comes down, no one hangs around
A loner 'til the end, until there's that magical spark
Awakening new loves promenading across this town

I know that I'm never alone in my home town
There's a friendly face with a pleasing smile, not a frown
Welcoming a loving heart ready to settle down
Everyone is friendly here in my small home town

Men with broken hearts tend to believe everything stark
When the sun comes down, no one hangs around
A loner 'til the end, until there's that magical spark
Awakening new loves promenading across my small town

THE FIRES OF MY HEART

The fires of my heartburn feverishly out of control
As my willow soul drapes the twilight
Hours of drowning in its own eternal hell
Awaken memories of my stories to tell

Turning up this torturous heat my body is beat
But my will remains strong for the one I long
Relieve my pain, let it be killed
Moments with you I'm eager to steal

The smoke rises hurriedly
Toward the Heaven's eager embrace
Where my love diligently dwells
As angels' breath bellows my sail

The fumes are ever so sweet,
A fragrance, I'll soon miss
Should I fail to seal the deal
Two hearts kindle as one and gel

Turning up this torturous heat my body is beat
But my will remains strong for the one I long
Relieve my pain, let it be killed
Moments with you I'm eager to steal

COLORS OF ALL HUES

A foggy red glow shades my eyes
Raging embers ignite deep inside
Roaring like thunder, rushing as ocean tides
Colors of all hues are destining to be seen
The light rains down hard and clean
A thick cloud of fog moves in and blinds
Hiding from view the fires battling inside
A tender rage that commits and binds

In a moment, in an instant time collides
Uniting two palpitating hearts with all ties
A want, a need pleasingly abides
Roaring like thunder, Lightning untamed
The light rains down hard and clean
A thick cloud of fog moves in and blinds
Hiding from view the fires battling inside
A tender rage that commits and binds

BLACKEN DIRT

Midnight's candles twinkle throughout the universe
Carrying my pains to an unmarked shallow grave
Issues unresolved will be my curse as I travel in the hearse
The lane is barren and rough, paved in blacken dirt
Whaling emotions swell massively, eager to burst
A stone crumbling heart is untimely late for a fresh start
Two shadows before my failing eyes, what could be worse,
Standing firmly to my left and to my right
Choices are many, regrets are few, no decision coerced
Ashes to ashes I'm lain back into blacken dirt

SUICIDE WAS CLOSE BY

Two hearts softly beat as one
Warm and tender not like stone
United our union will be strong
We'll never be left silently alone

Suicide was close by as I watched you walk away
Tearing out my love-sick heart and throwing it aside
How unsuspected the divide on this horrid stormy day?
Need I fall onto prayer or simply walk away

Suicide was close by like lightening it fled
The rush of my sigh extinguished the night sky
Twilight opened my eyes as I waved you goodbye
The only surprise untethered the tie you obviously surmised

PRIMARY

Blue is a color hot I perceive as cool
Red is icy cold burning a simple fool
Green raging jealousy unfurls the spool,
Purple heart I protect up top this stool

LOW DRAGON FUMES

Gone for such a lengthy spell
I'm returning to settle home
The fires that burned vigilantly
Have ceased to bewitch their spell
Coming back from once I was born
To rest among those familiar, I'll dwell
Low dragon fumes simmer short now
Each of my scales rains off one by one
The demons finally expelled
My wings are unfurled but no longer fly
For centuries, this story has been told
Each breath shows the fire extinct
My energies are limited melted to coal
Like all dragons, I've come home!
      I've come home to die!

Que Sera, Sera
My roots are well soiled
Fertilized, water and grounded
Que Sera, Sera
This old dragon is home!
I've come home to die!
But a bit of bite is left to be alive!
In this gentle flame

[I lost my scales in the tide
My wings drenched in the flood
My fire extinguished by holy water
Now, I've returned to the home
Low dragon fumes won't exhume
Roots stretch to no end are doomed
Worn conscious just looms]

INTER WOUNDS

Your blacken words are swollen with an evil vengeance
Your broken heart crumbles of coagulated blood
Your eyes bulging, ignite the fear within a lonely soul,
No tears of compunction shed to heal your inter wounds

What kind of unholy corpse are you?
No heaven, hell or earth would defecate you!
What type of punishment motivates you?
No incarceration compares to indictments served by you!

Your eyes of Kentucky coal reap nothing but revenge
Your thoughts twisted in murky soil hail vegetation
Your foul mouth spews the puss of low esteem, insecurity
No water to cleans your pain or redeem your shame

JUST WALK ON BY

When troubles brew, I court my blues
Harboring solace as I search for peace
The sanctuary I find in you carries me from troubling tunes
Harvesting solace as I discover your loving grace
If I should fall from the sky would you recognize me or
    just walk on by, walk on by

RECALLING MEMORIES

When I return to settle in silence blue
Rejoicing in the embrace of your peace
Where my sanctuary dwells forbidding rules
My harvest is vast as our love last, never to cease
Whaling my voice through the town of my news
Welcoming the charms of life, I'll continue to dance
Waiting for you to recognize that familiar tune
Where in an instant moment you feel thy grace
Recalling memories of our special place

WATERFALL

There is imprison memories in my mind I can't see
A chaotic world crossing the vast universe inside of thee
Boiling to erupt and let the hot molten lava vividly flow
Pouring baby deep dark secrets I never wanted to be exposed
Now! Now I open, I let go and just let it all go
A waterfall it floods drowning all compose, as I let go

Oh, waterfall rush down hard on me
Cleans these memories, set me free
I've done it all to appease the deed
Waterfall release my woes, show me the key
Rush your hot rain down hard on me
When it is all done let it all show

There's a darkness that no light can ever touch
The guilt I bear is great but it's never too much
The secrets I tell my friends are liquid gold
I'll not share with you such a powerful dose
I'll spare you depths of pain that goes and goes
I'll protect you from the turbulent waterfall, as I let go

Waterfall
Waterfall
Waterfall

There is no patience to bring a sense of peace with ease
Tolerance of forbidden memories engross thee
Eruption merely spoils the validity of what's sewed
Nothing I can do or say will honorably console
Now! Now I open, I let go and just let it all go
Cascading thoughts unleash their might, as I let go
    My Waterfall

OCCASIONS WISDOM

The hate of my soul taints the logic of my wisdom
As occasion lies fair altered in reverence
To the treasures of thy heaven whose gates waiver
Indicative of my unscheduled matriculation
I'm both pleased and astonished of blessings bestowed

Where heaven leaks, unworthy souls may seep through
Herald angels repair to diligently guard such entrance
Askew perception hands no solid judgment
Taxed of slave indulgence reaps uncontrollable greed
Occasions wisdom seldom redeems significantly to appease

Sorrow in my heart heralds to your call
Framed in the condolences of weak voices
In mournful woes, your spirit mulls
My fruitful love shall not part or stall
I'll aid decisions to assure your choices

Just spread your wings and kite high
Allow the angels' breath to bellow your sails
As tears swell in your bloodshot eyes
I'll remain your shoulder on which to cry
Know in the sigh my love will be your guide

As you cross the threshold of changing time
You'll not be left alone to bear what's gone
Family, friends will gather to bring you home
Unfurl the reservoir of sorrow tuck deep down inside
Release your deathly pain as your voice screams

It's difficult to let go of the one you loved so
Untimely it always seems of an uplifted soul
All seasons gathered to hurl their wealth
Dreamlike emotions forge in accelerated super stealth
If only you could awaken from this horrific nightmare

Beseech the nature of life for the moment will not linger
In an instant life blooms, in an instant, I feel its mighty doom
Love merely icing the avenue in-between seductively sweet
An illusion to distract one's thought prior to the blow
When the wealth is exhumed back unto the creations

I bear no anger when my heart sorrows and soul drowns
My compunction is diligent as I grieve (for one or many)
No dream state will solidify the reality of my deepest pain
The wealth of joy, love, happiness escapes, cease to exist
An occasions wisdom merely pampers this moment of solace

My windows are flung wide open to this world of breeze
Anchored beneath the arbor where the English ivy grows
Embracing the chaos as its tribulation withers to dry ash
Peace seldom visits a loner heart whose love has vanished
While acid rain washes away ill harbored emotions burning

DRAGON

Demonic eyes fire with hellish rage
Angrily gilded in ominous crimson nobility
As darken light all is perceived
Until lit by the truthful bright of day
No longer does righteousness
Bellow strong wind to sail forth my wings
Work harden steel scales gradually fail
Falling onto lifeless earth's rich soil
Decaying until fresh seeds are fertilized
And my weakness is far beyond recovery
My spirit dampens to such acknowledgments
With tail furled home, I head to hibernate, dwell
My fire extinct barely fumes puff of smoke
A meek whimper of self-pity bellows
The age and the ravages of time have consumed
The strength of my agile soul
I return to a familiar place to lay and growl
Until my time has come

SATELLITE EYE

I may be close by or a long way far
But no matter where you are
I'll always be watching you
Keeping you safe day and night
With my watchful eye
From high into heaven's
In the cold dark of universe space
I'll be purveying you with my satellite eye
Though I may not be close by
I'm always by your side
With my watchful satellite eye
Where time stands still, frozen
To hold my memories of you

I AM BLIND

Though my eyes have sight, I am blind
A wealth of information pouring into my corneas lenses
Need be filtered for me to see clearly
The pot of gold at the end of the rainbow
This is the inheritance of sins evolution's stained curse
Bestowed upon thee by the error of my ancestry
Adam and Eve
Though bards crossed centuries, generations
The translation was muddled in reverberating muck
A single grain of golden sand does bare truth
Allowing the purist of light to appease my regaining sight

My eager brain desires to process data's input in raw form
Yet; concurrently, it realizes the streaming bits
Are not all they appear as my eyes can not
      Believe one hundred percent the information
      They gather — the light is so bright and intense
The wash of purity is its own burden
As the fog grows ever deeper its thickness
Shrouding the shadows and distinct edges
How much more clearly the blind does see

THE DEAD COMMIT TO SIN

Morning sun streams through cracks of the mini-blinds
Waking to the excitement of another wild and crazy day
The noise, hustle, and bustle of the city dance about
Time clocks spinning round, round as day moves on
I'm headed down to Time Square to get some sweet
Sweet white sugar
Gonna drink her up like a bubbly pink champagne
Though I'm doing time, doing time of whiskey and gin
I bear no shame
As the dead commit to sin. As the dead commit to sin.
Zombies of trans-analytical suicide
A holy habit of pain
Tell me no secrets, tell me no lies
I accept the sole consumption of your alibis

The matriculation of my elated words
In each formed sentence brands the essence of
My pure thoughts
Screaming their release from their organic jailed prison
Whose bars lose strength with time
Merely a moment is for truth
To shine on bright, lighting this world in utter chaos
The shadows of logical thought
Bare no history of violence
As rage and resentment measure abound
I'm doing time, doing time of whiskey and gin

I'll not concede to any shame
As the dead commit to sin. As the dead commit to sin.
Zombies of trans-analytical suicide
A holy habit of pain
Tell me no secrets, tell me no lies
As I accept the sole consumption of our alibis

TASTE MY KISS

Under full moonlight, under full moonlight
My hunger ignites, an emotional hunger
Needing to be appeased, to fulfill the need
The need of my curse, my burden sin
Out of control my hunger always wins
Here comes night again like in my dreams
I'm roaming, stalking, hungrily on the prowl again
Through foggy dark mist until you taste my kiss

By wake of dawn, all my memories are gone
I wonder realities dreams as the sun races on
The excitement in my bones do hellishly pain
The agony of recalling my true name
Ummm, your aroma carries on the wind's breeze
As my body contorts I fall on bended knees
I'm roaming, stalking, hungrily on the prowl again
Through foggy dark mist until you taste my kiss

. . . until I taste your kiss

AT MASQUERADE BALL

At a masquerade ball
A room filled with friends
Though only a hand full are what they claim
Others latch on for the carousel ride
Pseudo mask displays their essence
A mirror of their true selves
As such fierce characters
Enjoy a deep southern promenade
Darken blood bathes this genuine scene
Lights choreographed like a motion film
Whirling mist rises from the deep
My hunger ravenously grows
As the libation fails to quench my primal thirst
The glorious glow of full moon shades me now
In hell, again I feel as if I'm home
As I surveillance, the grounds and roam
A sweetness rides on the night air
Aroma musk inundates flared nostrils
While I savor splendidly pink champagne
On diamond ice clinging its alibi
Jaded endeavors fever this mourning soul
Paining to rekindle structure a meet morning light
Performing a wavering penance of regret and indulgence
Border-lining both worlds of this life
One of mortal and one of a god
Parking is on the dance floor at a masquerade ball.

DROPPING SHADOWS

When the rain comes, it pours down, pours down
Blacken skies clue into the hazardous storms as
Bulking winds rodeo, trashing by and by

When the harvesting pain settles near the town
And the truth's shadow towers its weight heavily
Cowboy Up, drop your shadow and release your lace

Dropping shadows and secrets
Putting your life to the test
Harness your inner strength
And live the life you know best

Dropping shadows will ease the load
Dropping shadows will seed your soul
Dropping shadows will open your heart
Dropping shadows will warm your life

ENCHANTING CHARMS

Enchanting charms of my faculties
Appease the world and its sensibilities
Ignore the perplex of human complexities
Wreathed, staggered, and chafed by contemporaries

Suicide hearse engross my willing soul
Only I have the answers, only I can know
As wondering streaks inscribe thy brain
Love storms hard like a thunderous rain

Suicide eyes vigilance me
It's a masquerade shrouding thee
Fortunes made, fortunes lost
It's my consecrated soul required to redeem the cost

You can't hide from its sharp blade
The reservations have been fabricated
They say with liquid thoughts the world has concluded
But I am blind and my mind has been polluted

No shadows, nothing's there
Poetry's muse is left disrobed and bare
In this dream, words have no blush
I live in a world — of crimson and rust

The color of truth veils a conspiracy of silence
No derelict of romance will wrath turbulence
For constellations, shall retort true love
As I pursue my valued chalice love

I've trekked this earth, inch by inch
From firmament to persecution I missed not a stitch
Still, my soul gallivants aimless for limbos salvation
In an unforgiving world of lumber and obliteration

The moon, stars, and sun are darkening
Voices draped, mauled are summoning
Chills descend the distance of my frame
Leaving a nothingness, a shell with no name

Button fly dreams and shadowed mysteries
Are flavorful parfaits of poetic tapestries
Capturing truth on an amplified flight
I feel a movement taking me to new heights

My mausoleum is darker than the darkest Godless night
Everything creepy crawls in a swamp of delights
As I lay here now, digitally bound, life went unserved
Had I known what I do now, cremation would well serve

She dances where words haven't spoken
My little Khrystyan of spirit and motion
Ancient thoughts cast spells of darkness upon me
I remember a place . . . but it's escaping my facilities

Masquerades shed and reveal their disguise
Of hideous lies are deteriorating hellish demise
Murky vegetation reverberates its deceitful reign
Leaving me paralyzed — Brain Mad — insane

Simple is its prayer bewitching innocence's admire
Am I truly, brain mad? Do I dare, do I dare, a life so dire?
Incarcerated as I slumber in hellish lumber
I live in a world — like no other

The severity of my isolation collapse
Leaving me without a deadly corpse
Forsaken mediation, séance, or Ouija boards
Sanctuary shall never conjurer me back into your world

Existence is merely for my indulgence
Gay Chaos my dance of masquerade and belligerence
Frivolous and mundane is this sordid escapade
Concluding finality of my petrified confinement —

A solar eclipse and planetary alignment
Seal my fate and casket permanent.
Listen closely the wind chimes sing
Enchanting charms awaken winged things.

I toast with A Tequila Cocktail
I no longer remain under witching spell,
I have but a few more bards to tell
As you inject additional wind in my sail

I'm your candle in the wind
Guarding you until my end
Then I'll start all over again
Giving my loving heart absent of sin

For the time is the master doing me in —

CARAVAN

A caravan of rotting souls rip through the thick
Godless black of Satan's delighted night
Eagerly with evil, wicked vapor lusting
Ravenous for the defecating taste of sin
Forging into my asphyxiating world
These abominable demons pour from
Satan's sour nectar with vigor
Greater then Nigeria Falls
Leeching onto the tiniest strains of life
Their malodorous stench of centuries reeks fowl
Inundating with deteriorating emptiness
Collapsing time upon itself—stressing my will
The rifts wide gaping mouth
Violently vacuums in the badness of rich delights
A smorgasbord of gourmet prime
Iced in the sweet succulent apocalypse
I could not hear my own scream kite
When my blood streamed down the rough rocky road
For millions upon millions were screaming too
Vacating echoes pulsed from the depths of a pitiful well

HEAR THE LOVE

In screams of terror, I hear the love
Puzzled minds collapsing in fit full fear
High tea during witching hour toll
Ghost and goblins play demons game
The players are simpletons
The rules are inundated with decent

My eyes are dazzled as night awakes
Hypnotized by enchantments hovering
Though I'm blinded in this dark
I have a vivid splendid sight
Eager to witness the erasure of universal fear
I eagerly grasp for life—I don't know why
In screams of terror, I hear the love

There's no easy way to fight this consuming feeling
Daring to step through this night willing
Whatever it takes to survive—I'll be dealing
It may take my heart but it's my soul it's stealing

The earth beneath me quakes angrily
Leaving me with a failing appetite
In my screams of terror, you may hear the love
In the screams of terror, I hear the love
In the screams of terror, I hear the love

UNFINISHED

Today a be the day—my world will change
The news is on—the verbiage never change
The people and faces are different
But their issues and stories never change
The radio is blurring—the music doesn't change
The artist regurgitates—their palettes never change
Today a be the day—my world remains the same

NEITHER HERE NOR THERE

Flies gather vagrantly on the frail windowpane
I see a murder of Godless crows circling spiritedly
A dying clock ticks and tocks in the background
The annoying rhythmic dripping of water continues too
A burning, melting, scorching smell ultimately consumes
The room's last fresh air
Chills raise hairs on my strong arm suddenly
Hollow voices dance swiftly past my audible ears
No one is here, no one is there
An anomaly must certainly be
The sky is graying—a storm appears to be forming
Approaching
The television has come alive with its
Programming pixels, in and out
Something grumbles, something pops
As the lightning strike ignites charging my heart

Whatever idle thoughts form logic now is
Neither here nor there—in the end

NOCTURNAL

Reaming swells of lavish natural lust
Captivates the deviant of evil minds
Enduring suffers from their original sin
Their nature cursed to plague the masses
Redemption permanently allusive of their grasp

Shallow veils of pseudo display
Presents masquerade charisma and charms
Shadowing ills reeking of uncontrollable fear
Patching foolishly their heart of terror
Eventually a trimmer, a quake crakes the surface
Exposing casual glimmers—clues
Weighted holding down their facade—grounded

A devilish wicked evil beyond comprehension
That slithers beneath Godless blacks of the night with
Blazing eyes of the nocturnal

CONSEQUENCES

Deteriorating, eroding souls laid the wealth of these frail tracks
Roughly the Zeppelin train has reached its last destination
And the consequences it solely bears
   Meek or bold
   We all must die alone
      A pile of rusting bones
      Just antique skeletons
      Laying in consequences

SKELETON BONES

Skeletons storm through the cobweb shields
That were holding—in archival reserve—my darkest secrets
Relics of decades' past, left long forgotten
Yet remaining in reaming ocean swells of my thought processes

Dormant, idle, they lay at rest, hidden
Blanketed beneath a cloak of Godless black,
Draped imprisoning mold, mildew, and
Thick rusty iron strings of heavy cobwebs—
Supposedly buried in the depths finality forever

Hallow mass eventually soars
As sprockets of time forge and turn
Each bit and byte meticulously encrypts
The building bones of chattering skeletons
As they violently regain morsels of life
Until truth radioactively combust and explodes

The genuinity of my image endures
As my skeleton bones collapse
It's a fatal but wrathful demise
The present matured—now grows steadily dimmer
The past rematerialized—prospering in its clarity

SENSES

I love the sweet taste of depression in the morning
The thick fragrant aroma of a lingering suicide
Awaiting to appease my wickedly strong carnal thirst
As my ravenous hunger abounds this fluid night

I bath in the lush marsh pulling you in its quicksand
The hellish stench invading every tiny orifice
Awaiting the tainted libation my taste buds so crave
As my stomach grumbles, heavily for your prime meat

I walk the shadowed path politely hidden from direct view
The dense draping fog cloaks my wild spirited presences
As I deeply inhale your confused vulnerable essence
As the clock chimes, down unto your timely expiration

I love the tart taste of depression in the morning
I love the salty scent of suicide in the afternoon
I love the foul acquisition of your soul in the evening
But what I love most of all is the adventure of our senses

Feel my cold welcoming touch
Smell my hot bated breath
Ear my wicked hypnotic words
See my world of elated delights,
Taste my sweetest nectar

PROCESSION

Worldly deeds soon bleed
Weeping sorrow of salty tears
Ready to be planted
A grave resting deep in the ground
Watered for the soul to move on
My heart dare not cry
Nor do my eyes leak tears
Emotion has lost its compunction
As my blood has coagulated,
All you see is skeleton and bones
I stand here firm, alone
A pillar of strength
The weakness merely is hidden by fear
Don't scrutinize too closely
Or you may uncover wet tears
My skin has leathered
In this passage of time
As my heart sorrows for what?
I feel soured—tainted
As this day kisses night
Though the marriage will not last
Between life and death
It's what's in-between that needs to be seen
I'll not matriculate
Into idle contemplation

Deciphering my universe
For when I welcome my demise
I'll plant my feet on fresh barren soil,
Repeat it all again
When it is my turn
To step from life into the cloak of death
Do not grieve for me
I have left with no regrets
Or sorrows to heavy my mortal heart
And weight down my immortal soul
Just sing the music with joy
Praise my exit into the unknown
For I'm positive my journey will be swift
I'll cruise this excursion through
Purgatory
Like a strong summer breeze
My testicular fortitude
A not whimper these final test
When your rain nourishes my heart
It will melt away the hardness
Until you see it glow,
Then you'll know I've
Made it home—alas!

COLOR MY SOUL

Hues wash over me like jealousy and rage
Burning lava of the sun my harden cage
But when cool tides rush and bath me calm
It's your undying love that colors my soul

Giving me sense, a need to belong.
Thunder roars and lightning strikes
Fire consumes my appetite
As your soothing hues shower down over me,
The world eludes all sensibilities

I'm forsaken of all color for the sake of society
What's your love doing for me, but offering destiny.

Entering in large jeans
Your harden body invades my dreams
But when the sun and moon collide
You color my soul like only I know,
laying here by my side

Wild desire conquers my heart
Finding Heaven as we play the part.

BARREN RUN

I know of a church where sinners go
Back in the wayward sticks with people chanting low
The road is torturous and heavily weeded so
Paved with hellish vagrant demon's empty souls

Barren Run is the place no good people go
The righteous stay very far away from this I know
For they seek not to soil their integrity so
Their Bibles held tight though clearly shows

I know of this evil place out on hypocrite's row
Where the wicked country folk find no substance to sow
Only because the elders have forewarned me of its tow
I dare not tread as summer breeze push and blow

Barren is the vacant run of this forbidden road
No salvation can ever come from Satan down below
The sinners march to no just end murmuring low
I have sworn to never ever give them over my soul

The heart of Barren Run is blacker then Kentucky coal
Their lashing tongues contaminate the winds with every blow
You'll find no shelter of innocence's I have been told
For their demeanors are unseemly and centuries-old

Hypocrites and thieves of barren souls' worship at Barren Run.

STRUCK HARD BY FATE

I knew a girl, fate struck her hard
Out for a Sunday family joy ride
Having a jolly good time
With her husband and beloved son
When suddenly was heard a crashing noise
The lights go Godless black
Waking on a hospital gurney, bright lights overhead
Looming voices blurred, fading in and out

This girl I knew, struck hard by fate
She's no longer the women she used to be
Her heart and joy were instantly stolen away,
No matter how much she prayed
She's not the woman she used to be
She's not the same today
She'll never be the woman she used to be
Her heart and joy were taken away

I knew a girl that lost all her dreams
Fate can be so cruel when her storm set in
A blessing and heartache like an avalanche hit
Concurrently the news of rolling stones continued to slide
The grim ripper took her son that day
The doctors found cancer, her husband they saved
One year later fate stepped back in,
Her beloved husband died.
A year to the day—my friend

This girl I knew, tread dangerous times
Romancing depression and dark suicide dine
Her heart and joy went leaving lost and alone
Though she cursed and prayed the heavens above
Her world was dark and all but gone
People promised time would ease her agonizing pain
But the truth, the hurt remains ever the same
There is no cure for what fate dealt out
Listen close and you can hear her silent shout

AN URN'S JUST FINE

Give me not a liquored casket with comfort and flair
Give me the bare essentials for I'll just be laying there
Give me not wall to wallflowers and plants galore
Give me a tombstone so people can remember me forevermore

If this be to much trouble for you my dear, I do declare
Cremation to ashes and an urn suits me just fine, jeers
For wherever I may be at rest or scattered here and there
I'll be forever watching you dearly, this I boldly swear

Give me not a black suit and tie because you feel you must
Give me an Armani Tux and Gucci shirt with French cuffs
Give me not a parade of avalanching tears come crowd at the dust
Give me your sweltering pregnant heart my endearing Muff

If your weaken tears fall before the priest chants my heaven's call
Lay in weep until you find a shoulder waiting for you in the hall
For where ever you masquerade I'll remain at your beckon call
I'll be forever watching you dear, my questionable squaw

FOUR WALLS

Four walls, a Holy Cross,
All the things I adore most
Guilt sharp as double edge sword
A faucet of Holy Water blessed
No wonder my mind is such a mess
I hear Rosary and Keys clang
Music of torturous—sounds of pain
Shackled and chained my blood came
Crystal thorns of Christ come at a price
I have this fever high and low
Struggling demons desiring my only soul
Righteous I be because I bare not the cold
Watch my heart of coal burst
      Into a diamond boldly bright
Piercing through the thick darkness
You can grasp what is always right

NEARLY ALIVE

Hammers strike and spark as nails drive in ever deep
Construction sounds inundated my reverberating ears
Outside my window, a pile of mahogany wood slowly dwindles,
On the brightest of days when I'm two steps closer my grave
A coffin is poised mid-center my master room
Finely tailored, hand-oiled mahogany wood and brass finishing's
Laced interior of delicate white silks with pillow and mint
A cough here and there, a failing body weak
I dare not close my sleepy eyes or be buried quickly alive
The vultures are swarming my bed-side
Awaiting a chance to stake my ailing heart
A stake to my heart beneath a gentle pale moonlight
The chance they eagerly abide
     as hours and days move gingerly past
I know this feeling so very well and
     I'm not yet willing to fly to my final rest
Until such time I'll remain nearly alive!

VACANT

Once upon a time the gods shinned
    their blessed graces on me— yes me
Though it took the masses of over
    40,000 angels to left my mortal finger
You spoke three words that extinguished
    all their wills and mine— yes mine
What pray tell beseeched you to
    dagger my smiling heart
    causing me to leak tears,
    shed my crimson blood onto
    slate gray colored stone floor
Sucking me dry, reminding me
    daily with a permanent stain
The gods raged with fuming anger
    ascending messengers and workers
    to foil, make right
But your heart would not melt your soul of
Godless black to beckon warm light
Upon the deduction
    a curse placed would shadow your remaining life—

        No happiness will grace your path
        No love will bless your temple
        No fortune will prosper comfort
        Your generations to follow will bear the graves
    the burden of this path you paved

Eternal damnation will bind you
    eternally as the gods will shun
    energies of you
Lay in the coldest depths
    beyond all galaxies
    in a forgotten corner
Where those such as you forever reside

    Not even a memory as you have no name to speak

Should time permit you to contemplate
    during your incarceration
    of agonizing pains
    beyond depths of any comprehension
    or wildest of imaginations
Any compunction has been well abandoned

Your sunken wells are barren
    with full delinquency—
    do not seek to seep a single tear
    thinking a reprieve be granted from compassion
You have reaped sour fruits and must lie
    in the spoils, you devised,
Blanket yourself from true eyes—that witness
A heart of chilling stone cannot be chiseled
    into fine sculpture beauty

From a master's worn hands
    when its soul is utterly vacant
I will not shelter my harboring anger
    for I'm the victim
Unknowingly, I tread foggy marsh quick-sandy sod
    of insatiable appetite

How noble my reasons to shower the wealth?
    of my justifying love
How genuine my words to comfort and
    adorn you as royalty
How meek I fell on bended knee to grace
    you with my servitude
Merely to have you bequeath the ravages
    of your maximum devastation

I ripped away from my scared fleshed,
I peeled away layer upon layers
Until my skeleton stood erect, bone dry,
    then soldiered forward
Trailing any remaining filth in the passage of time
    to appease the
Last leeches deprived and emaciated

This lone journey has left my spirit
    undoubtedly vacant

SILVERY TONGUE

Sweet resonating words crossing your heart shape lips
Sounds gingerly warm and intoxicatingly inviting

I hear melodies strum as each word of thought flows
Flawlessly off your silvery tongue's bladed tip

How cavalier your presence that leaves me feeling
Heatedly engrossed yet stone-cold, frozen

What book of plethora thoughts do you scribe to when your
Fevered ink fails to bleed obediently along
   the raw silken page

Do I dare speak in rebuttal or initiate a battle until it renders
A full scale, full-blown war—
Neither party is inclined to surrender
   a white flag of defeat

STONE HEARTS

Stone hearts never catch fire
Nor burned by the flame
While gnawing on the green relish of liars,
Cloaked in mockery of languishing souls
Tainted rose may open and weep its morning tears
Petals fall to decay, thorns bite a taste of fear
Then close tonight's lone velvet
Moonflowers blossom to their glory
Praising the heaven's twinkling in the twilight
Full bloom trumpets their gentle song of silence
Pristine white as bright as the glorious full moon above
Though trapped in this luxury of beauty
Stone hearts cannot catch fire
Nor burned by the flame
Royal blood of day cannot trespass or
Tread upon evenings blatant flesh

WAYWARD CHILD

Trust your inner light and thoughts
   my abandon wayward child
Don't allow the uncertainty of your heart
   to bleed on my Italian marble floor
Permit your idle soul to flow freely
   with ease of fresh running spring
For your wealth is not found intangible things
   but in the beauty of an untarnished love
Your trials have been devastatingly long,
   they have mauled their massive weight on you,
   you are forever better—stronger
Shelter, not those harboring ill feelings of neglect
   they offer nothing but trauma, confusion,
   agonizing pain
—you'll concur in retrospect—
Relieve your thrusted burden,
   leave behind all that cast you barren
   value is in the quality of genuine thoughts,
   feelings, emotions
Weep not salty tears of regrets as you have done no wrong
Forgive the idiot whose character is a desolate wasteland
I am here, I am here to take your crusty hand
Because there are small steps to uncover
Salvation in a man my wayward child is futile

SIMPLE SOUL

Love be such a simple thing I'd truly like to share
Standing before you now simple and heartily impaired
I voice my feelings—emphatically do declare
It's the simple things that really show I care
I'm but a simple soul with a holding prayer

My heart kites with the love I have built inside
You need only open yours so the two may forever tie
For the innocence's of two beatings as one never lie
Our union is blessed with the meeting of our eyes

Love be such a simple thing I'd truly like to share
Standing before you now simple and heartily impaired
I voice my feelings—emphatically do declare
It's the simple things that really show I care
I'm but a simple soul with a holding prayer

My soul soars freely without worry of deceit and alibis
I'm but a simple man holding true my word to abide
Walking down the shore, hand in hand, I want you dear forever
     by my side
In this bliss and your fresh kiss, I feel the rushing tide

Love be such a simple thing I'd truly like to share
Standing before you now simple and heartily impaired
I voice my feelings—emphatically do declare
It's the simple things that really show I care
I'm but a simple soul with a holding prayer

My eyes present no gypsy's chant to curse or hypnotize
My thoughts are pure as I desire to be your only guide
My words are honestly sure—genuine for everlasting time
For I'm but a simple soul who's willing to turn a blind eye

Love be such a simple thing I'd truly like to share
Standing before you now simple and heartily impaired
I voice my feelings—emphatically do declare
It's the simple things that really show I care
I'm but a simple soul with a holding prayer

    I am but a simple soul with a holding prayer
    I am but a simple soul with a holding prayer

CORPSE

A fanciful corpse
Decays in blessed earth
Scorpions dance in Fall dress
Chattering along the tracks

IDOL HANDS

Idol hands a devil's helper
Consuming neighbor's goods
Coveting is thought to sin
Just the thought is a crime
Of forever idol hands

LIGHT

The light is equal to the dark
Each a scale of balance
Though the two meet
They shall never kiss
Shadows lie in-between

CHAMBERS

What a man gains
From treasures of love
Rest in his heart's chambers
What a man gains
From the pleasures of his thoughts
Rest in his hands of sin

DRAGONFLIES

Dragonflies with translucent wings
Speeding by as time ticks mildly
In the splendor of not knowing
The jar will be your prison cell
Until you die
Or my amusement is no longer appeased

SOUNDS

Drip, drip, drip
I hear your Prince nearby
Splashing in the watering hole
Jumping from lily pad to lily pad
Not a care in his little world
Drip, drip, drip
He is so sopping wet
Do you dare kiss his amphibious lips?
Listen for other sounds

GRAVE

My grave be shallow
Dark and deep and cold
My mausoleum be hallowing
Shadows, foggy mist, bone-chilling
My toast echoes and bellows
Colleagues no longer social

IN THE NAME

Genius borders the dance of insanity
Anticipation burdens the nervous system
Radioactive the shell releases energy
Yet, an image of God is formed from clay
Alabaster stone marks the first excursion
Delivered the sterling knight of honor and valor
Respect the courage and strength of nobleman
Utter his name for the sweetest
Taste upon your tongue
Recite his propelling words in pride
Yiddish is not a language he speaks
In the name

WITNESS

The journal of life is unfolding
Before the eyes of masses
Blinded by the emporium showers of confusion
That dazzles empty words and promises
A poor boy sired by mid-eastern
Now rising to great power
In the greatest of western land
The benefactor of Satan's domain
Prepare to receive your commerce mark
Bear it proudly barren ones
In the towns, square turn circle
Take your barren souls and run
Run quickly down that barren run
Find his welcome church of
Heathens and hypocrites

Witness their Godless blacken eyes
Witness their tainted rotting hearts
Witness their empty dead souls
Witness their foul waging tongues
Witness their barren, forsaken, vacant shells
Witness the hells of their cold fiery touch

The sour taste sears leaving your mouth
Dry and malty — cottony dry
Simply entices you in to what's to come
As your will unjustly diminishes
Beget no trust in the son of man
For he will do you nothing but
Grave harm with his pregnant words
Soiled by a mere acquaintance
Your acquisition is forged solid,
Your term may be permanent

No whimper will free a condemned man
In trial or tribulation
Whether justly or bogusly accused
You must maintain a strong constitution,
Accept nobly your sentence
Until the wealth of your sword is sharp and true
Unleash your own fires, your own brimstone
Chant the validity of your own words
Cement their value into every
Orifice and crack needing healing

No hyperbole can soldier against a valid truth
Behold my logic by decrypting the fallacy
Surveillance the playing field and
Gather in unity the masses
For the raven has diligent eyes,
A righteous tongue can slaughter by
The tens of thousands
Its Nemesis
Endure the battle and conquer a
Pregnant war

CONTEMPLATIVE PROSE

Arrest all action, absorb the silence
Allow the hustle and flow to freeze
Awaken your eyes to the abundance around
Stroll through this glorious moment
Bathe in its breathtaking beauty
While it may last,
Just prior the last few seconds pass
Hear nature's chorus as the full choir of
Motley birds sing
Feel the soft docile Summer breeze
Dieseling your spirit
See life renew with changing seasons
Touch rich soil dark and nourishing,
Taste all ripe hue fruits—exotic
Just prior to speeding back into
The hustle and flow of a frivolous mundane world
Time stands still in the reflective contemplative pose for one
For you are the air that I breathe

LOOSE THOUGHTS

I stare blankly at these cinnabar colored walls
      heavy in Tuscan flair
My thoughts idle and rampant concurrently
      the synapses dare
The walls expand and contract as if they are breathing,
As if they are living—alive
Sounds of quiet are overcome by daily noises fair
The plumbing, the air, the cracking floors
Everything that settles with age,
Grows louder and more noticeable
As night moves in so briskly
The stairs cascade in a downward spiral
The room is not queer but all too familiar
My grasp for innovative thoughts—sanity
Attempt to stream my words onto a recycled paged
My inner artist remains allusive
My active brain has stalled, drawing a blank,
Awaiting the light bulb to burst into its freedom

BEYOND THE STONE

I value the wealth of seeds that I've sewn
Reaping immeasurable harvest beyond
Any platinum or gold
My bushels are overflowing I respectively know
I gather this bounty before it all goes
Time is a bastard it headlines the show
Weathering the storms, surviving droughts toll
I soldier up, manned the shields, high and low
Battle my nemeses as their energies blow

I extend my hand with love from my soul
As my pregnant heart permits its lava to flow
While my mind wraps around memories not long ago
These treasures now are to have and to hold
I embrace the wealth that cannot be bought nor sold
The ties are clearly strong and centuries-old
I'll trek this path no matter how long
For its wealth, last eternally beyond the stone

I will keep in my memories as a favorite song
Every precious lyric right where it belongs
When war has ended at the last bell's dong
I'll mourn in darkness forever slow
Weep not on your travels as you leave the cold
I bow my head, fingers entwine and fold
My words will be true and kind as your story be told
For I value the wealth of seeds that I've sewn

There is a world somewhere out there beyond the stone

DROWNING IN A SEA OF MY MEMORIES

Standing with my head hung down low
Standing in a cold Kentucky summer rain
Thunder rages, rattling my fevered brain
Dazed, confused
Drowning in a sea of my memories I come up for air
A vision I see but you're not there
I shake off the wetness, brush off my never-ending pain
When lightning flashes past
      I swear I heard you call my name
Voices bounce to and fro these long nights without care
This torture test I no longer want to bear
Sympathize and understand what's driving me insane
It's all in the moments when this avalanche came

Sunrise 'til sunset
I'm drowning
Drowning in a sea of my memories
The pain hurts piercingly deep
But I no longer bleed
I'm drowning
Drowning in their depthless sea
(nothing I do now will appease)

Running for my life through the heavy fallen snow
      I've no one to lay blame
I could spin a story or two but that would be cowardly lame
Balancing the scales of good times, bad times isn't fair
Because of our suicidal dance of Russian roulette
      waited for the dare
Reality is what I make it . . . Who says it must be sane?
Time, time keeps moving the clock's hands
I keep holding on to what we shared
Drowning in a sea of my memories I rush up for air
Hesitating a moment — a mere frozen second —
      I'm lost in nowhere
In the Sahara Desert, I'd have a mirage of a dream
Do you truly comprehend what I desperately mean

Sunrise 'til sunset
I'm drowning
Drowning in a sea of my memories
The pain hurts piercingly deep
But I no longer bleed
I'm drowning
Drowning in their depthless sea
(nothing I do now can please)

A SIGHT TO BLIND

Thoughts rampant wildly via the chambers of my mind
Bordering where no sane man dares to ever be
Fallacies and logic are my mixed accord
Surface thoughts to common are barred here now my Lord
Tread my venue should you venture
      to comprehend my kind
Seize this moment tittering tightrope of genius and insanity
Frivolous and mundane vigorously consort
      merely to settle the score
Black velvet never beseeches or begets sweet emptiness
Behind a barren scarlet door where
      foul greenish ooze resides
Humanly ecliptic I witness a sight to blind
Words are allusive but thoughts never stop
Depthless wells continue to swell until its zenith
The frozen instant of epilepsy stalls time for me

DEAD TO SPEAK

Whispers haunt me throughout this endless night
Ghostly eerie sounds of spirits now and past
Attempting to conjure premonitions
Aiding in their indirect communication
At first, these unwelcomed shadows stirred some fright
Ghoulish energies lingering in a thick foggy mist
Prevailing with deliberate disturbing commotion
I enforced my presence and demanded my motion
One contemplates it will arrest when day releases it light
Forego this invalid notion cause it's merely a rouse to mask
Angels, demons, entities gravitate toward promotion
Permit the dead to speak to settle their damnation
Queer sounds are their words forming sentences
     'til one hears
The solemn cries of prolific loneliness and despair
When the dead speak, the vibrations are weak

PRAY TO MY SHADOW

Answers appear out of nowhere before my sight
A plethora of questions abound in thoughts right
I showered my bountiful love merely to cater
Now I'm left alone to break and shatter

My profound questions are left on an unanswered diet
My constitution accord may initiate an uncontrollable riot
Does it really matter who gets hurt or severely battered?
My feelings are damaged, confused and scattered

How many times can I pray to my shadow in the twilight
How many times can I romanticize thoughts of sunset delights
How will I recognize the one love that madly truly matters?
How will I really know love will be with me in the hereafter

Refrain:

    How many times must I pray to my shadow
    How many times must I romanticize what matters
    How will I forego being so shallow?
    How will I love being in the hereafter?

FRAGMENTS

White	like	virgin
Black	Icarus	melts
Ink	euphoria	flows
Stain	welcomes	soul
Red	blood	boils
Dare	tentative	target
Be	demise	now
Bold	blue	sky
Blatant	highs	mountains
Words	blue	ensue
Suicidal	lows	linger
Romantic	sails	bellow
Raven	cave	Dracula
Corpse	skeleton	bone
Scarlet	bare	heat
Envy	raw	natural
No	no	no
Reprieve	compunction	exoneration
No	no	no
Absolution	entombment	mummified
Journey	ends	immediately
Of	and	for
Curiosity	wisdom	knowledge
Fate	faith	kismet
Intervenes	intertwine	bonds

Fragments initial three stanzas are meant to be read from top to bottom first column, second column and then last column. The fourth stanza is read from left to right as in standard reading practice. Fifth stanza starting at top should be read right to left. Additional stanzas are read at a diagonal using a 1,2,3 or 2, 4, 6 count sequence. Example: column one = 'White', column two = 'Icarus' and column three = 'flows'. *White Icarus flows.*

HOME IS IN MY HEART

I have silver and gold,
Rubies and diamonds
To keep me from getting cold,
A pick of any lover
Money to burn,
I'll not be the one to suffer
Lessons I've to learn,
I've no shame to cover
My glass always half full,
It's the life I choose
The full moon in night's lull,
The cycle continually shows
    the way life goes

Leather and lace —
Heavy metal and chains
I've pleaded my case,
I'm not crippled of lame
A piercing tattoo in a secret place
Experience etched in the lines of my face
But it's the memories of you
I long to have and to hold

Home is in my heart
Flooding with a river of love
U & I R A start
Together with giving the world a show
A mauling hurricane
Rushing love to a higher plain
In this unique comfort
I recall your gentle name
Holding on to my memories
Cures what ails me
Cause it is a natural remedy

NO FRIEND OF MINE

Mary Jane, you're no friend of mine
I have nothing to do with your kind
As far as I care you may eternally fry
Stay your distance don't bother to try
Those that seek your bogus company
Are useless losers and unfortunate needy
Take your five jagged fingers, discover suicide
I don't care how or where you die
Mary Jane, you're no friend of mine
— never a friend of mine
It doesn't matter how persistent you are
You're disaster causing heaven's shooting stars

      Mary Jane, you are no friend of mine
      Mary Jane — never ever a friend of mine
      Your enticing ways I'm forever blind
      I'll never have anything to do with your kind

— see the sign — __1__

HALF A WORLD

Listen to the whippoorwills
    Down goes the sunset
        Burning up the sky

On sharp edge of the horizon
    Lay itself to solemn rest
        Blatantly awakening a new dawn
    Elsewhere

Half a world in total darkness
    Half a world is wonderfully luminous
        No in-between for spirits to fly

Listen to those fiery tongues
    Forked with sour words
        Mauling intently its lies

A dull edge cuts worst
    Dripping nemeses in honey works best
        You'll find kindness is everywhere
    Elsewhere

Half a world in absolute blackness
    Half a world in human likeness
        It's in-between where your spirit finds mine

COLLEGIATE

Remuneration is a gratuity
   when you matriculate into my fastidious world
Prolific in academic ivory contemplation
   learning commemoration
No vacancy for hyperbole as logic
   arrest and impedes fallacies
Judiciously malodorous constitutions
   beseech exoneration to no avail
I bequeath my plethora consorts
   to evaluate the substance of your character
Execution my only recourse in
   decimating your hedonistic proclivities
      Knowledge is the ultimate succession

DAYS OF —

In hot lazy days of brilliant Summer
The sun bears down blistering hard and
Burns me deep inside
Warming my charred heart aglow
As typhoons tides push my love
With fevered romantic flow

In cool hazy days of motley Fall
Gentle breeze carry many of song
Awakening a rejoiceful sigh
Cradling my spirit to show
As a whirlwind engrosses my faith
I'm standing steady to go

In freezing shady days of grey Winter
Clouds gather bearing a wealth of blanketing snow
Just my frozen thoughts reside
Chilling the bone core of my soul
As the rain pours down washing away my care
I'm left standing with a bucket of black Kentucky coal

In warm maybe days of romantic Spring
The world reawakens with blossoming floral's and
Sap juiced budding trees aside
Jointly my body quivers to and bows
As old life erases and new life springs forth
I stall merely a moment before consuming the whole

SILENT MIRROR OF MEMORIES

Staring blankly into the silent mirror of memories
Beseeching noble thoughts to beget and nurture
A child of superb wonder and admiral strength
I implore the gods of wisdom as a servant scribe
My deduction copulates with a plethora a creative muse

Awaiting the mastery of miraculous miracles
To part, the seas and the heaven's so
I may bear witness their inspirational light
Release my processes, my proficient muse and
Free thee from the vast entombment shadowing me

My human words flavor a mix of sweet and sour,
Bittersweet merely to tantalize a mortal mind
With like Halloween treats and shallow tricks
Though some discover the taste a touch to darn salty
For their discriminating upper crust palettes

The bite is generous when it tangos with tangy
An I reminisce with the silent mirror of memories
Bequeathing my last drawn breath for poetic enlightenment
My muse and the literary gods relinquish their virginity,
As my fountain of ink rivers across the parchment again

THAT'S HOW I ROLL

My thoughts are the instrument
        that beget me to feel great agonizing pain
Others nonintellectual opinions
        have no bearing value for whom I no respect
Words may hail mauling down around me with loathing
But my strength and integrity
        does not drown in their quicksand
I'm the mass of superheroes in a single mortal
I lease no vacancies in my mind to store clutter
That's who I am, that's who I will be, that's how I roll

FACELESS WORDS

We are all death in disguise
Faceless before a world of truth
Two shadows in lives dance
Acting on a global stage

Each script unique
With a story that repeats
Generation after generation
The longing is always the same

Even when the names do change
We live this life
Wanting the same things
To love and be loved

We open our heart
And close it to the hurt
The carousel is always the same
We come forth nude
Into this world with a promise
As we die alone into earth's
Ashes

Our tears wash away the pain
Our tears cleanse the ills of a soul
Our tears mend a torn heart
For
We are all death in disguise
Faceless as we walk as shadows
In a world that never really sees us
Or hear our faceless words

BLANK

I do not understand why I cannot acclimate

The wealth of logic sporting solid valid reason

My mastication of wonderment

Does not erode the invisible force field encompassing me

I comprehend the levity of continued isolation

Undermines my grand design

Yet, I'm incapable of penetrating

The solidity of this transparent barrier

I did not matriculate this fiasco knowingly

Therefore I am left BLANK

THE PAST RESOLVED

Sorrow ran through my heart like a raging river
Tainted with the darken bleakness of despair's fair
Awaiting time to provide solace and contemplation

I implored my vigilance to emerge anew
To forsake the romance of final release
Though its peace remained platonically charming

The presence of my calm resolve simmered
Purposeful and steadfast I breakthrough — Free —
Leaving the past well behind in pause

My clear eyes determine the vision, leaves my past resolved
Literally erupts, disseminating my idealized strength
Bathing me exquisitely in noble character

As I soldier forth the battle is lain to rest,
The war is extinguished and ceases to exist
For I have indeed — the past resolved

KENTUCKY CLAY

A plethora of azure sky and cotton clouds
Drift freely across mountainous mounds
Striking vivid imaginations ravenously ablaze
Floating aimlessly in a causal dream-like daze

We are two sailboats adrift aimlessly
Sailing toward the other on a vast sea
Our lighthouse beacons us to the golden shore
On our journey, kismet bounds us forevermore

My love is just like Italiano Stone
It's long and hard and everlasting
That is the way I felt when you came
Everything I ever needed was in your name

I found my home in solid Italiano Stone
My heart palpitates solid like Italiano Stone
I found my love in your Italiano Stone
You're made of that exquisite Italiano Stone

Poetry Ends

www.ingramcontent.com/pod-product-compliance
Lightning Source LLC
Chambersburg PA
CBHW050851160426
43194CB00011B/2106